SECOND EDITION

The Insider's Guide to Commercial Real Estate

Cindy S. Chandler, CCIM, CRE, DREI

Dearborn

A Kaplan Real Estate Education Company

This publication is designed to provide accurate and authoritative information in regard to the subject matter covered. It is sold with the understanding that the publisher is not engaged in rendering legal, accounting, or other professional advice. If legal advice or other expert assistance is required, the services of a competent professional should be sought.

President: Dr. Andrew Temte
Chief Learning Officer: Dr. Tim Smaby
Executive Director, Real Estate Education: Melissa Kleeman-Moy
Development Editor: Christopher Kugler

THE INSIDER'S GUIDE TO COMMERCIAL REAL ESTATE SECOND EDITION
©2013 Kaplan, Inc.
Published by DF Institute, Inc., d/b/a Dearborn Real Estate Education
332 Front St. S., Suite 501
La Crosse, WI 54601

Printed in the United States of America

ISBN: 978-1-4277-4432-6 / 1-4277-4432-7
PPN: 1556-4002

contents

Part 3   **Careers in Commercial Real Estate   117**

Appendix　**Due Diligence Checklist**　**164**

Welcome to the exciting world of commercial real estate! You know more about it than you realize. Do you shop? Do you enter office buildings? Why do you select those stores and professional offices? Perhaps you own or rent commercial space. Why did you select the property you did?

Unlike residential real estate, which is based on personal desires, commercial real estate is leased or purchased by businesses who select the space they do because it is right for their business. Is there a reason a grocery store wants to be on a certain corner? Why do all the drugstores seem to be near each other? Is one corner better than another is? Is the location of the skilled labor pool critical for a large manufacturer? The answer to all of these questions is "Yes!"

When referring to real estate, the term *commercial* can mean different things in different places. Most people use it to refer to nonresidential property. In some cases, the brokerage of large multifamily properties, such as apartment complexes, is included as part of commercial real estate because here brokerage is considered investment sales. The purchaser is typically an institutional investor, such as a real estate investment trust (REIT), pension fund, or a life insurance company.

In this book, we'll begin with "Getting Started," which covers getting you into the business, the different commercial areas, what to expect, the tools you will need, and some career options. You'll find many examples throughout the book. These examples are true stories, but the names and some details have been changed.

We will learn the basics of different types of developments. We'll focus on office and retail properties because they are the most common for newer brokers and investors, but we'll also discuss specialty properties, such as industrial properties, and those developed for institutional uses, such as government properties. What is important in each? When does location matter and when does it not?

We will investigate what a real estate investor (could be you) and other types of buyers look for in a commercial real estate investment and look at the different types of investment real estate. An individual investor investing for his or her own account will look at an opportunity differently from an institutional investor, such as a pension fund, life insurance company, or REIT.

Because all real estate begins with the land, we will spend significant time reviewing land use, conditional contracts, and due diligence. Why is a soil test so important? What's a watershed? Are the wet-lands on the site good news or bad news? We'll see.

Once you have a basic understanding of what commercial real estate is, we'll move on to more advanced topics that will give you an insider's look at how the profession operates, from contracts to financials and more.

What types of contracts are involved in a commercial real estate transaction? We will cover the key terms of a sales contract and learn what is important in a commercial lease. Once the property is developed or purchased, someone needs to manage it. So we'll cover the essential elements of a property management agreement.

We'll learn the buzzwords and the arithmetic. The math of commercial real estate can progress from very simple to very sophisticated, but the math is nothing you can't handle! We'll learn how to use capitalization rates to estimate values; compare apples to apples using net present value calculations; and look at time and value of money using an internal rate of return.

If you can finance it, you can sell it. It is true that if a commercial property is attractive to a lender, it will attract more buyers. Few buyers want to self-finance. We'll look at the different sources of funds and determine how much an investor can borrow based on a property's cash flow. We'll create pro formas needed for financing a property and study commercial real estate loan basics. From there we'll put on our underwriter's hat, look at a property as a lender would, and determine how much we can borrow.

Do you need a broker, or are you a broker? What type of agreements will you need to execute? How is the broker paid and by whom? Is it different for selling versus leasing? What questions should you ask a broker when interviewing him or her? If you are a broker, what questions should you ask a buyer, seller, landlord, or tenant before signing the agreement? Answers to all of these questions are covered in the third section where we look at commercial real estate careers.

Perhaps you want to try your hand at development. We will review the process, the steps, the pitfalls, and the upside of developing real estate. We'll create the financial pro formas, explain how to complete a feasibility analysis, look at the timelines, and determine profitability.

In commercial real estate, it's important to know how to "walk the walk and talk the talk." Half the battle of understanding the fundamentals of commercial real estate is knowing the terminology. As in many industries, commercial real estate has its own language. We will demystify the secret language of commercial real estate and get you on your way to a successful career.

Excited? Well, let's get started!

—*Cindy Chandler, CCIM, CRE, DREI*

acknowledgments

Cindy S. Chandler, CCIM, CRE, DREI, has been in real estate for more than 30 years. She has her own consulting and training company, the Chandler Group, and has worked for numerous organizations in the areas of investment real estate, syndication, strategic planning, management, and marketing. She was formerly associated with the Cogdell Group, the Crosland Group, and the Paragon Group with responsibilities in commercial real estate in the areas of syndication, development, brokerage, property management, and training.

Cindy has served as an expert witness in several real estate litigation matters. She has authored numerous continuing educations courses taught throughout the Southeast. In July 2011, she was appointed to a three-year term to the North Carolina Real Estate Commission.

Some of her REALTOR® leadership positions include the following:

- National Association of REALTORS®
    - 2013 Chair, Commercial Legislation/Regulation Subcommittee
    - 2011 RVP Region 4 (Kentucky, North Carolina, South Carolina, and Tennessee)
    - 2010 and 2008 Liaison, Commercial and Business Specialties, Extended Leadership Team
    - 2008–2011 Executive Committee
- North Carolina Association of REALTORS®
    - 2006 President, 2005 President-Elect

Some of her past community and civic positions include the following:

- Chair of Zoning, Charlotte, North Carolina
- Chair of Planning, Charlotte, North Carolina
- Chair of Zoning Board of Adjustment, Mecklenburg County, North Carolina

Based in Charlotte, North Carolina, Cindy travels throughout the Southeast teaching commercial real estate classes, though she prefers to spend her off time at her place in Hilton Head, South Carolina, with her husband, Tom.

Many people were instrumental in the development of this book. The following people were a tremendous help in clarifying and refining this and the previous edition of the book:

- Chuck Byers, GRI, CRB, Pioneer Real Estate School
- Herbert S. Fecker, Jr., CCIM, Ed Klopfer Schools of Real Estate
- James (Jim) E. Howze, Advanced Career Training, Inc., Houston, Texas
- Cynthia C. Shelton, CCIM, CRE, Colliers International

Basics

Getting Started

overview

Perhaps you are selling homes and want a change of pace, or you are working for a bank and need a new challenge. Maybe commercial real estate just fascinates you. You are thinking of a career in commercial real estate, but where do you start? This chapter will give you the steps to get started. ■

l e a r n i n g   o b j e c t i v e s

When you have completed this chapter, you will be able to

■ list differences between commercial and residential real estate,

■ list professional organizations which offer commercial real estate education,

■ list some technology vital to the commercial real estate industry, and

■ describe options for a real estate career.

■ Starting a Career in Commercial Real Estate

"Why do you want to be in commercial real estate?" is the first question I ask of those who come to me for advice. The following are some of the common answers I receive:

■ "I want to make lots of money."

■ "My family has dabbled in it."

■ "I have some family money to invest or land that I would like to develop."

■ "I know someone who is in the business."

■ "I heard about it in school and want to know more."

■ "I used to own a business and leased from a commercial broker."

■ "I was in banking, lending, architecture, etc."

The motivations are quite different, and in many of these cases, those seeking information already have an advantage but may not know what to do with it (or that they have it). This is when they turn to me for advice. The advice I give them is directly related to their answer to my "why" question.

This book should help you get a better handle on the advantages and disadvantages of commercial real estate for you, and the book will help you decide whether commercial real estate is right for you. But let's start with the one question everyone has in mind: the money. Do you make more money on commercial real estate than on residential? Let's try some math, as seen in the following examples:

Sample Residential Transaction

Agent sells $300,000 home.

Agent co-brokers it with another firm (the listing firm).

Agent's firm gets 3%.

Agent gets 65% of his or her firm's share.

Agent's commission = $5,850.

Sample Commercial Transaction

Agent leases 5,000 square feet of space with a three-year lease at $20 per square foot.

Agent co-brokers it with another firm.

Agent's firm gets 3%.

Agent gets 65%.

Agent's commission = $5,850.

What about selling a $50 million mall? Likely, you won't be doing any of those types of transactions right away, if ever! In any case, even though you can make a lot of money on big deals, they take much longer to put together.

Years ago, one of my commercial real estate transactions took three years to put together (and it was nowhere near $50 million). I had marketing and promotion money in it—plus hundreds of hours of time—and if it had terminated (which it threatened to do several times), I would have been out that money. Here's what happened.

I was a new development manager with a commercial real estate development firm. I discovered a tract of land held by our company in the suburbs. When I asked about it, I was told it was not being developed—the site was too green. *Too green* means that it is too soon for whatever development is being reviewed—in this case, a shopping center. It was felt that there weren't enough nearby homes to support the shopping center.

I was allowed to take on the project. First, the grocery store and drugstore I had initially counted on both backed out when they found out about the greenness of the project. I found new tenants but then ran into problems with building codes and zoning ordinances. On top of all of that, the contractor found bad soil under the grocery site. Luckily, I found a cost-effective way to import soil from a neighboring site.

In the end, I was able to lease the corner site (called an outparcel) to a fast-food franchisee at a very good rate, and that made the rest of the center profitable. We sold the center a couple years later at a very good profit to an institutional investor. However, had any one of the many complications caused the project to fail, my company and I would have lost thousands of dollars and hours of our time.

While most nondistressed residential transactions usually close within two months of signing the contract, commercial deals do not. Even the 5,000-square-foot lease in the example above could have taken as long as six months or more to get done and paid. Then again, it may have closed in a few weeks.

The shopping center example above illustrates that while it can be frustrating and somewhat risky, commercial real estate can also be very satisfying when a deal finally goes right. Another advantage to the commercial field is its variety.

■ Types of Commercial Real Estate

In commercial real estate, there are even more avenues and more distinct types of avenues than in residential real estate. Let's take a look at the following major areas where one can find a career in nonresidential real estate:

- ■ Office
- ■ Retail
- ■ Industrial
- ■ Institutional
- ■ Investment
- ■ Resort/recreational

Keep in mind that these areas overlap, and there are often subspecialties within each category. For example, in larger markets, a broker or developer may specialize in only highrise office buildings in a certain part of town. In small markets, to survive, most brokers do a little of everything—even residential—as the market does not have the depth to allow specialization unless they do most of their deals out of their area or handle a very large area. We'll discuss most of these categories in detail in Chapter 2.

■ Professional Organizations

Given the many categories of commercial real estate, training resources may initially seem more limited than for residential real estate or other business fields. However, there are vast resources; they are just industry-specific and not marketed nor directed toward the general public or even the commercial real estate generalist. One must be aware of the numerous professional organizations in commercial real estate to know where to look for training. Also, many of the commercial real estate publications are somewhat technical, filled with industry jargon, again, meant for those in the business. Some organizations may even restrict information so that only its members may access it.

Many of these organizations are listed below. Some of them offer advanced education and designations, and those designations are also noted in the following list:

- CCIM Institute: Certified Commercial Investment Member
- The Counselors of Real Estate: Counselor of Real Estate (CRE)
- Institute of Real Estate Management (IREM): Certified Property Manager (CPM), Accredited Residential Manager (ARM), and Accredited Commercial Manager (ACoM)
- REALTORS® Land Institute (RLI): Accredited Land Consultant (ALC)
- Society of Industrial and Office REALTORS® (SIOR)
- National Association of REALTORS® (NAR)
- International Council of Shopping Centers (ICSC): Certified Shopping Center Manager (CSM), Certified Marketing Director (CMD), and Certified Leasing Specialist (CLS)
- Building Owners and Managers Association International (BOMA): Real Property Administrator (RPA)
- Urban Land Institute (ULI)
- Commercial Real Estate Women (CREW)
- Commercial Real Estate Development Association (NAIOP)

Many other commercial-related organizations and groups exist, and they typically serve the advanced or corporate commercial real estate practitioner. Several of the above organizations are also comprised of experienced practitioners, but because most offer educational programs available to all, they are a good resource for a new practitioner.

■ Career Options

For many years, I taught the real estate courses needed to obtain a state real estate license. While most who enrolled thought they would sell homes—either new construction or general brokerage—many were encouraged to try commercial real estate when they saw all of the career opportunities in it. Let's look at some of those opportunities.

General Brokerage

Commercial agents can represent buyers or sellers, assisting with the sale of a commercial property. These agents are typically independent contractors, not employees of a company, and work on commission. Another part of the business is leasing, and the agent can represent the tenant or landlord in negotiating a lease. Depending on the size and depth of the market, an agent may specialize in a certain product type—retail, office, industrial, or a certain geographical market, such as a city, county, or region.

Development

An agent can work in several areas, such as actual development, project management, and leasing. The development staff purchases land and builds something on it—a shopping center or office building. Perhaps an existing building or center is purchased to renovate. The developer arranges financing, negotiates the "anchor" (large, important) tenant leases, hires the architects, contractors, et cetera, and supervises the process until it is completed and the tenants move in. The development team may consist of a project manager who manages the development process and a leasing agent who handles the leasing. They may be salaried, paid on a commission basis, or both. Other specialists can be part of the development team, too, and they are usually paid a salary plus incentives.

Property Management

Once a property is purchased or developed, it needs to be managed. The property manager handles the day-to-day operations of a property—staffing, contracting for services, repairs, maintenance, et cetera. For these services, they earn a fee. Individuals employed by property management firms are usually paid a salary.

You'll learn about each of these career opportunities in more detail in Part Three. First, we need to cover the basics of the field so that you can decide where you fit in. Because brokerage may be one of the most common ways of breaking in to the commercial real estate field, and because the broker needs to know a little bit of everything, most of the information in this book will be presented from a broker's point of view.

■ What to Expect

What can a person expect as far as compensation, hours, and so on, as a commercial real estate broker? It depends. If the market is strong and the agent well connected with products or buyers, the sky is the limit. Because of the nature of commercial real estate, it is difficult to describe the business of the average broker. Unless a new broker comes in with products or buyers or is placed at an active project, it may be months before a deal is done and then another few months before it is closed and the agent is paid. In some areas, the most common practice is to pay part of the commission when a lease is signed and the balance when the tenant takes occupancy. In other areas, all the compensation may be paid when the tenant takes occupancy. With a sale, commission is typically paid when the deal closes.

Many brokers make in the $75,000 to $150,000 range; some make far more. Some will tell you that they made $250,000 one year and $75,000 the next.

Different professional organizations cite success statistics of their members' commercial real estate business. For example, the National Association of REALTORS® reported that the median gross income of their commercial members responding to a survey was $86,000 in 2011. According to the survey, the median age was 57 years old and 66% of the respondents had a college degree or higher. The median number of transactions was seven, with a median transaction size of $2 million. Forty percent of the respondents were members of other institutes, societies, and councils, such as the CCIM Institute or the Society of Industrial and Office REALTORS® (SIOR).[1]

The SIOR reported that SIOR designees completed an average of 30 transactions per year, valued at $30.1 million per member, representing an average 1 million square feet of space.

The CCIM reported that their designee mean age was 51, with a candidates mean age of 47. About 76% are men, with an average of 19.5 years of experience in commercial real estate. In 2012, the median number of transactions completed in the past 12 months was 17 with a median value of $7.5 million.

---

1   National Association of REALTORS®, "Highlights from the 2012 Commercial Member Profile," National Association of REALTORS®, www.realtor.org/reports/highlights-from-the-2012-commercial-member-profile (accessed March 13, 2013).

Commercial real estate can be a cruel business. It takes time to build a good reputation and only minutes to ruin it. It also takes time to develop the savvy to be trusted with the bigger deals. Training (outside the national designation programs) is hard to find.

Although it can be a tough business, commercial practitioners receive many intangible benefits. They become a part of the community, are aware of development going on, and know who is at the forefront. Commercial real estate involves so many other industries—banking, investment, construction, architecture, engineering, et cetera, that the active commercial broker quickly becomes a known figure in the area and may have an influence on the growth and development of the community. For those in development, driving by a building he and she created adds a certain continuity and permanence to life in our rather disjointed and disposable society.

■ Tools You Will Need

Depending on your goals, the tools needed may increase in complexity, learning curve, and cost, but the following are the bare bones.

Computer

If you are considering a career as a commercial practitioner and if you expect to work with clients who have any level of sophistication, then a notebook computer, smartphone, or tablet is a must. You may wish to have a desktop computer in your office, too.

Software

Contact management software helps you keep your notes in order and allows you to contact multiple prospects when a property is available. You will also need word-processing and spreadsheet software. I suggest you also have some type of database software. Bundled software such as Microsoft Office has most of what you will need. There are more sophisticated contact management systems, such as Sage ACT!, that you may want to try.

Financial Calculator

Make sure that you have a financial calculator or a similar program on your smartphone, tablet, or notebook that allows you to make quick financial calculations—and that you know how to use it. Hewlett-Packard financial calculators are popular with commercial brokers and have been used in CCIM courses. There are many other brands of calculators available. Check them out and use what is easiest for you.

The CCIM currently uses the CCIM Excel Calculator, an Excel spreadsheet, in its classes in lieu of a handheld financial calculator. Technology and processes continue to evolve, so stay abreast of what is new and most efficient.

Website

Commercial real estate clients expect the broker or the broker's firm to have a user-friendly website. You'll need the capability to display any listed properties, allow users to perform searches, and have your company's information (including contact information) somewhere that is easily found. In addition, you may want to include information about the economy and articles about topics commercial real estate users would find interesting, such as tax law issues.

Social Media

Websites such as LinkedIn, Facebook, and Twitter may be useful when properly used in business. They allow the commercial real estate licensee to form networks of users and contacts.

■ The Commercial Real Estate Culture

Keep in mind that most commercial practitioners are different from residential agents in many ways. Most commercial firms are small and offer little or no training, and commercial agents are typically hesitant to share any information. You have to ask, and even then you still may not get what you need. Commercial agents usually work alone, not in groups, jealously guard their potential client list, and don't typically use a multiple listing service (MLS). In some areas the commercial real estate market is like a secret society, where you need to know the password and secret handshake to get in. And once you're in, commercial agents still don't freely share information. Many don't participate in regular meetings or commercial real estate group activities. They usually don't show property at night or on the weekends, and they typically don't have their photographs on their business cards, both common traits of the residential business. Some exceptions to all this is the practitioner whose market is smaller and does both residential and commercial and the practitioner whose market is in a resort location, where many clients come on the weekends to view property and enjoy resort amenities.

In lieu of the MLS, many commercial firms use commercial information exchanges (CIEs), which show commercial properties listed. The CIEs do not offer cooperation and compensation like MLSs. Examples of CIEs include the National Association of REALTORS®' site (www.realtor.org/commercial/) and LoopNet (www.loopnet.com). Most brokerage firms have their commercial listings on their sites.

When dealing with businesspeople, brokers may need to dress more formally and learn the language of their investor clients. Residential agents need to look and act professionally, but because they don't want to intimidate their buyers and sellers, they may have a more casual appearance. It all depends on the market.

Some commercial properties are not advertised. Why? Well, as seen below, there are several possible reasons. The property may not be actively for sale. In other words, the seller might sell it only if the right deal comes along. The seller might want to keep the upcoming sale quiet so as to avoid rattling the existing tenants. The commercial broker may not want to work with an inexperienced agent. Experienced commercial agents know who handles what in their market and who to call to find out who handles what they need in others. The data needed to determine if a buyer client is interested in a particular property is confidential, and a seller is unwilling to release this type of information to people they don't know or buyers who are not qualified. For these reasons, it is difficult for a new agent or new investor to break into commercial real estate.

Because the broker is still the gatekeeper of the information (potential available properties or potential buyers), the broker guards it carefully. There are fewer commercial properties than homes, and while the dollar volume may be the same or even greater in a market, there just isn't the need for as many agents. Commercial firms are not as large as residential firms, and agents act independently from one another.

The duties of commercial agents may vary from those of a residential agent—the commercial agents may or may not get involved in the financing, inspections, and so on. Their main task may be to locate suitable property, and it may often be unlisted. Because many times they will have to find unlisted properties to meet a buyer's need, their primary task may be just that. Some buyer clients have their own sources for funds, inspections, legal advice, et cetera. At most these buyers may ask the agent to do some follow-up or coordinating. Other buyers may need much more time and advice from their broker.

The interpersonal skills needed for commercial brokerage can also differ. While a residential agent needs to be personable and have knowledge of community things, such as school districts, the commercial agent will need to have a better grasp of the community's economy, tax districts, and zoning laws. In many cases, the commercial agent will need to perform a financial analysis, requiring skills in lease interpretation, investment criteria, financial strength of tenants, et cetera. The commercial agent may never have a face-to-face meeting with the decision maker, or time spent together may be limited. If it's for pure investment, the buyer may not even visit the property but send a representative.

■ Assembling Your Team

For commercial brokers or investors to be successful, they need a team of professionals they can rely on to provide information, advice, and counsel. Discussed below are potential team members that a broker or investor should consider for each project.

Accountants

Some buyers and sellers need financial advice on the acquisition or disposition of their property. Typically, it's outside of the broker's expertise to offer tax or financial advice. It's best for the client to talk to their own professionals. However, it's important that the broker stay involved in the deal so that the accountant will not be making the final decisions on the transaction. Offer to meet with the client's accountant to answer questions and to stay in the loop.

Appraisers

Most lenders will ask for an appraisal in order to feel comfortable with the loan. The appraiser must be approved by the lender and will follow the lender's instructions, while being paid by the buyer. At times a seller may want to order an appraisal in order to establish an asking price. It's important that the appraiser be experienced in the type of commercial real estate being considered.

Attorneys

Buyers and sellers need legal advice. Unless they hold a law license, brokers are not allowed to give legal advice, draft documents, create deeds, and so on. Many legal questions come up during a transaction, and, with proper involvement, the broker can ensure that the attorney becomes a deal maker, not a deal breaker. It is critical that the attorney be experienced in commercial real estate transactions so that timely and accurate advice can be rendered.

Engineers, Architects, and Land Planners

In the case of development, redevelopment, or even leasing of a property, the buyer may need the help of an architect, engineer, or land planner.

Lenders

As with most business transactions, in a commercial transaction, most participants need financial resources. The lender may be a construction lender, an acquisition lender, an equity lender, a permanent lender, or a combination of these types of lenders. It is important that a broker have relationships with all types of lenders. Buyers may have their own sources of funds, but a lender can assist a broker in preliminary valuation or be a key resource in the eventual financing of the property.

Other Consultants

Depending on the transaction, other specialists may be needed to handle certain areas. Following are a few issues that might require a specialist:

- Rezoning/land
- Historical designation
- Traffic/Department of Transportation
- Environmental
- Business brokerage
- Specialists such as physicists (for example, when building medical facilities with sophisticated X-ray equipment, the walls must have shielding and a physicist will provide the specifications)
- Information technology

The Broker's Role

As members of the team, brokers help the investor by locating property, particularly unlisted property, and they help other brokers by doing the same or by bringing the buyer to the deal.

The brokers bring the buyer and seller together. Many times, the broker finds unlisted property that meets the buyer's requirements. Some use an MLS for commercial properties but most do not. Therefore, the broker must go out and find suitable properties for the buyer to consider. The broker may or may not recommend professionals to use, such as an appraiser, attorney, or engineer. Much of the broker's role depends on the type of transaction and the needs of the buyer and seller. In some cases, a broker may bring the buyer and seller together, then back out, according to the instructions of their client.

We will discuss how a broker does this, and how the compensation and cooperation agreements are done later in Chapter 8.

■ Taking the First Steps

Let's say that you are either a successful residential real estate agent or a businessperson looking to change careers. You are not sure in which area of commercial real estate you'd do best. You have business experience and you know people (we'll call these folks your "sphere of influence"). What should you do? I give everyone the following advice.

The First Steps

Step 1. List everyone you know in commercial real estate.

Step 2. Call all of your relatives and closest friends and list everyone they know in commercial real estate.

Informational Interviews

In Steps 3 and 4, you begin to conduct what are known as "informational interviews." You are not seeking a position because you don't know what you want yet or where you may fit in. Most of us are somewhat clueless at the beginning stage, and to ask for a position when we are clueless is a mistake and can perhaps make us look bad. Looking bad is not the way to begin a new career that depends on reputation and business savvy.

Step 3.   Start calling. First call those from your list you feel will give you some time. Ask for only 15 minutes of their time. Explain that you are only gathering information, not seeking a position at this time.

Step 4.   Conduct the interview. During the interview, ask the real estate professional how he or she got started and what advice they would give a newcomer. Ask for a brief overview of their business and their industry, and ask if you can borrow or have some industry publications, usually found in their reception area or office library. Before you leave, ask for two or three names of other commercial real estate people you should talk to. Ask this person if you can say that he or she referred you (this can really open doors). Thank the professional for his or her time. Send a follow-up thank-you note a few days later. Send a physical note unless you know they will respond better to an email. Trust me, a hand written card will stand out from a sea of emails.

Narrow Down and Dig Deeper

Continue to call those on your list for informational interviews. At some point you will begin to eliminate areas of commercial real estate and start honing in on those areas you are becoming interested in.

Step 5.   Narrow your search and research further. When you think you have narrowed your search, research industry-specific websites. Read the organizations' publications and get to know the jargon, types of projects, and key players.

To get even more insider information that will help you get started, visit company websites and look at projects done by local companies or those being brokered by the companies you are interested in. Ask questions about these projects to ask that company or others in the industry. Also, attend as many commercial real estate classes as you can. Not only will you learn, but you will also probably make your best contacts there.

Step 6.   Know the details about employment. Get an idea of compensation structure. Some positions are commission only; some may be drawn against commission; some may be salaried. Decide what you can live with and what you can't. Unless you have something really unique to bring to the table (e.g., you're the heir to the Walmart business empire), you will not be in much position to negotiate. Feel free to try (there's usually a little wiggle room), but remember that others are seeking the same opportunities as you.

Step 7.   Begin the interview process. You are now ready for serious interviewing. Narrow your final choices down to no more than five. Unless you are in a very large market, commercial companies will know exactly who is in the market and whom they have talked to. Just as with commercial properties, commercial professionals don't like to have their candidates "shopped." Hence, you need to narrow your list.

At this point, you may begin to wonder whether you should go with a developer or a general broker. Unless you have a product to market, you should start with someone who does. Starting with a developer allows a new broker to learn the product and the market with the safety net of having a "captive product." Eventually, the brokerage community will know you, and you will know them through your marketing of your developer's real estate. Once you have some experience behind you, you can decide what you should do next.

If you decide to affiliate with a brokerage firm, research the firm as you would any company. Will you be competing with the other brokers in the office, or does everyone have a specialty? Is there someone there who will mentor you? Will you fit in?

Step 8.   Get the job. Call your contact person back for another meeting. Explain that you have talked with many professionals, have narrowed it down to a particular field (retail, office, etc.), have visited some of their deals or listings, and have specific questions. When you meet, ask your questions, share what you have learned, and ask what opportunities his or her company has.

Keep in mind that most commercial firms don't have "openings," but create slots depending on need or opportunity.

Explain what you can bring to the table. Remember that the company is interested only in what it will be gaining, not what you will. Don't spend too much time talking about your wants, needs, and desires unless specifically asked, and even then, keep your reply brief.

Finally, if you have an inside connection, use it! If your father and the company owner are golf buddies and you have decided that you can do well there, go for it! Most opportunities are created. As Cynthia Shelton put it, "It's normally who you know that gets you in the door, but it's what you know that will keep it open or keep you there."

Establishing Yourself in the Field

Okay, you got a position. Here's how to establish yourself in the commercial real estate business.

Step 9.   Maximize your exposure. You are probably not doing any deals yet, so give yourself something to do. Send announcements to everyone you know and everyone you talked to during the informational interview process. The announcements should state your company information and your position. They should invite the recipient to call you for their commercial real estate needs. Attend every commercial real estate event. Get involved in civic, charitable, and government affairs. Get on a city or county commission, join the Rotary Club, or get active in a political campaign. The key here is to maximize exposure. Don't spend too much energy where other, more established real estate professionals are active (unless you want to ally yourself with one of them). You want to be "the commercial real estate person" in your organization. Get into a "leadership" program. Join one or two commercial real estate organizations and get active early. It's easy because these organizations are always looking for workers.

Decide how social media will best serve you. Are your future clients using Facebook, Twitter, or LinkedIn? There are so many sites, and keeping them all current and interesting can be a full-time job. Look around and see what other successful business people are using. Be creative, but above all else, be discreet and professional. A poorly thought out party posting on Facebook can severely damage your professional image.

Step 10.   Use the brokers you know. Offer to help an experienced broker in your office either for free or for a very small cut. Offer to do the broker's grunt work—work as a runner, put up signs, measure space, or hand out flyers. Have your supervising broker create a training program for you (because it isn't always easy to set up such a program, don't count on this one). Meet with other brokers in casual settings (such as over a meal) and learn about their products. Have two or three brokers who will mentor you and whom you can call to ask questions and get advice from.

Step 11.   Keep learning. Ride around and view commercial property. Mark a map with areas. Take photos. List occupants and owners. Create a resource list of lenders, appraisers, builders, architects, and engineers who you can bring in on a deal to help you close. Talk with them often and understand their businesses. Attend every commercial real estate class you can. Also attend those classes that relate to your business. Finally, start working on a designation, such as those referenced earlier in this chapter.

Step 12.   Ask for help. And whatever you do, if you find yourself in over your head on a deal with a client or customer, don't try to wing it! Get help. "Goofing up" a deal can terminate your career quickly or at the very least, label you a rookie, which can have the same effect. Everyone will know. Because commercial real estate professionals are a small group, it doesn't take long for news to spread. Someone—hopefully your supervising broker—will help you when you ask for help. Commercial brokers may compete with you to get the listing, but once you have it and need help, commercial brokers will be there for you. Even if the broker takes the credit for "saving the deal," it's much better than losing your reputation along with your client who will not only be unhappy but may take legal action.

■ Summary

We've looked at the steps to get started in a commercial real estate career. You know what to expect, the tools you'll need, who you want on your team, and so on. In coming chapters, we'll go to the next step—types of properties and buyer types.

case study	**Personal Assessment**

This personal assessment should get you thinking about where to direct your efforts in getting started in commercial real estate.

Before beginning your career as an agent in commercial real estate, first ask yourself the following questions:

1. Where is my expertise?

   _____

   _____

2. Whom do I know, and who will buy from me or list their property with me?

_____

_____

3. What kind of income do I need?

_____

_____

4. Where will I get my training?

_____

_____

5. Why am I choosing a career in commercial real estate?

_____

_____

If you want to be an investor, ask yourself the following questions:

1. Why commercial real estate?

_____

_____

2. What subfield of commercial real estate do I understand?

_____

_____

3. Who is going to help me?

_____

_____

4. Where will my investment capital come from?

_____

_____

5. Can I afford to have it tied up for an extended period of time?

_____

_____

6. How much money can I lose, and what is my risk tolerance?

_____

_____

7. What are my investment goals? What returns do I expect?

_____

_____

8. How do I know my goals are achievable?

_____

_____

■ Review Questions

1. When considering a career in commercial real estate, you should consider
   a. who you know.
   b. what you know.
   c. your monthly financial needs.
   d. all of these.

2. When asking for informational interviews, you should
   a. ask for a job.
   b. emphasize who you know.
   c. learn as much about the company as possible.
   d. disclose how much income you need.

3. A difference between commercial and residential brokerage may be
   a. the hours worked.
   b. the type of information known.
   c. the type of client.
   d. all of these.

4. After interviewing the first time, you should
   a. send a handwritten thank-you note.
   b. send a thank-you email.
   c. do nothing until you decide which avenue you'll pursue.
   d. call to thank the interviewer.

5. To find suitable properties for a buyer, the best resource is
   a. a multiple listing service (MLS).
   b. a search based on the buyer's criteria.
   c. other brokers who deal in similar product.
   d. both a search based on the buyer's criteria and other brokers who deal in similar product.

chapter two

Types of Properties

overview

Before you can decide where to start working in commercial real estate, you need to know more about the choices. In this chapter, we will look at office and retail properties and study the traits of each. Our discussion might spur some creativity to help you decide where you fit in the world of commercial real estate. ■

learning objectives

When you have completed this chapter, you will be able to

- describe the different types of products,
- describe the effects of employment on real estate, and
- describe key characteristics sought by buyers and tenants.

■ Key Terms

1031 exchange

Americans with
   Disabilities Act (ADA)

anchor tenant

big box

building code

community shopping
   center

cottage/single tenant
   office

demographic report

employment base

foreign trade zone (FTZ)

neighborhood shopping
   center

pension fund

power center

real estate investment
   trust (REIT)

regional center

right of first refusal

zoning

■ Offices

There are many types of office buildings and developments. Building owners may or may not be tenants of their own buildings. In either case, they will be concerned with purchasing a desirable office property. In this chapter, we will look at different types of office buildings and users in some detail.

The following are some of the requirements of typical office users:

- Visibility from the main roads
- Convenience to area amenities (restaurants, shopping, etc.)
- Proximity to public transportation (bus routes, rail lines, etc.)
- Convenience to compatible businesses
- Easy access
- Proximity to airport, courthouse, interstate, and the like, depending on the nature of the business
- Pleasant setting (park-like setting, highrise status, etc.)
- Proximity to the homes of the workforce
- Proximity to the decision maker's home
- Taxing jurisdiction
- Pro-business municipality (tax credits, zoning, sign laws, etc.)
- Strong tenant leases
- Amenities in the building or complex
- Utilities and technology
- Security
- Parking

Employment Trends

In many markets, workers are not willing to travel long distances to work, especially if there are other employment opportunities closer to home. As businesses are locating nearer to where people live, some industries are finding it challenging to find qualified workers as businesses closer to the employees' homes have the advantage. Finding a suitable **employment base** is frequently the number one criteria for a business looking for a location.

When a business is considering locating (or expanding) in an area, it will seek incentives from the local and state governments. Incentives can range from special tax treatments and cash incentives to employee training.

In addition, many traditional industries are moving out of the United States, leaving hundreds or thousands of workers unemployed. Since the 1990s, we've seen the decline of textile, automobile, furniture, and other manufacturing businesses in the United States. When an industry leaves an area, it not only causes unemployment but jeopardizes other businesses that supported the industry or its workers. This downward cycle tends to continue. In addition to unemployed workers, loss of industry leaves empty office space—sometimes in a market where the space cannot be easily released.

Some examples from my home state include the furniture industry and the textiles business. With both moving from North Carolina to countries outside the United States, warehouses and factories have shut down. Businesses that provided services to these industries (e.g., dye manufacturers, equipment renters, makers of foam for upholstered furniture, et cetera) have also suffered. Further, unemployed or underemployed workers spend fewer dollars at retailers.

Types of Office Developments

Cottage/single tenant.   Freestanding small buildings fall into the category of **cottage/single tenant offices** (see Figure 2.1). They may be part of an office park or true stand-alone buildings. There are pros and cons with offices such as these. Cottage/single tenants may locate in converted homes in an area now zoned for business.

Figure 2.1 | Cottage Office Example

Take a moment to consider who might want to buy one of these properties. Typically the process starts with the end user. Small business owners may like the feeling of having their own building. Because parking may be difficult to provide, we need to consider how many employees and how many customers would come to this location. Service providers such as architects, engineers, surveyors, and appraisers might be good candidates. If parking and access are good, a small doctor's or dentist's office might fit in. In cases such as these, we look at location—location of the owner/buyer and the location of the owner's customers.

Now, what's the downside? If the building was built as a home, not a business, then the layout may not be efficient for typical office use. As stated above, parking may be an issue. While the **zoning** may be appropriate for office use, there can be issues with other ordinances and regulations. The **Americans with Disabilities Act (ADA)** requires that businesses, among other things, be accessible (see www. ada.gov). The **building code** is different for a house than it is for an office. There may be neighborhood restrictions. Certain businesses may not be permitted in that structure. Before buying or marketing a cottage/single-tenant property, check all avenues—zoning, building code, business licensing, et cetera.

Small, suburban office complexes.   These might be one- or two-story buildings that have multiple tenants. These have a variety of users depending on the demographics of the area and other choices business users have (see Figure 2.2).

Figure 2.2 | Lowrise Office Example

While the trend to work closer to home affects the desirability of small office complexes, a tenant must also consider what other businesses and amenities they need to be near. If they have clients they meet with regularly, they would want to be convenient to them. Maybe there are suppliers they want to be near. If the employees travel, then proximity to the interstates and airport might be most important. Another consideration is convenience to their customers.

Suburban offices can be susceptible to fluctuations in the market and demand for space outside of the central business district. They may be inconvenient to city or county offices, the courthouse, and public transportation (e.g., bus routes and rail lines).

Investors may purchase small office complexes. Investors will look at several things but will base most of their buying decision on either the current strength of the tenants or the future potential of the property—either stronger tenants or future redevelopment. Investors will also consider the overall office market when determining the price they are willing to pay.

Depending on the quality of the property, it might be a good candidate for an IRS **1031 exchange**. These exchanges use Section 1031 of the Internal Revenue Tax Code, which allows tax deferral under set circumstances (see Chapter 3). Markets and demand for certain properties change, but there may be little property for sale in certain price ranges being sought by buyers looking to exchange. In that case, the property should be marketed to brokers who have clients looking for exchange property. Another source of 1031 exchange buyers is real estate attorneys and accountants. There are companies who act as qualified intermediaries for 1031 exchanges, and they have clients looking for exchange property.

A tenant candidate for small office complexes (as well as any of the other office properties) is the local, state, or federal government. Government offices and county or municipal services might need a location outside the central business district.

Midrise office or an office park. These properties share many qualities with lowrise office buildings. Midrise buildings average five stories (see Figure 2.3)—in some areas, a five-story building may be considered a highrise—and are typically not in large central business districts (CBDs) because CBD land in larger cities is usually expensive and needs higher-rise buildings on it to be profitable.

Figure 2.3 | Midrise Office Example

Highrise office. This category depends on the market. A highrise may be seven stories in some markets, while in other markets it may be much higher. Building Owners and Managers Association International (BOMA) defines *highrise* as 25 stories and higher, though the qualification may be determined by height in feet versus number of stories (see Figure 2.4).

Figure 2.4 | Highrise Office Building Example

Note that different sources define *midrise* and *highrise* various ways. There is no set number because when talking about a building, a broker will cite the number of floors and, depending on the market, the building may fall into a midrise or highrise category.

In cases of headquarters of large companies, one of them might have interest in a high-profile building. For significant amounts of space or when considering developing or redeveloping a highrise building, be sure to contact your economic development representatives to make them aware of what you have. The economic development representatives (associated with the local chamber of commerce or a group formed regionally to promote business) are in constant contact with businesses considering relocation.

The first call when selling office properties (unless the broker is required to keep this confidential) is to the current tenants. If there is an **anchor tenant** (a large user of space), that tenant may be the best prospect. On the other hand, knowing that the building is for sale might worry tenants and create a lease problem. Always check leases to see if such a tenant has a **right of first refusal**, which means they have the first opportunity to buy it, if it is for sale.

■ Retail Developments

As with offices, a retail developer looks at what retail tenants want, and the developer bases location decisions on that. In some cases, the retail developer will not commit to a site until a major retailer has agreed to be part of the development. Let's look at what retailers find important. A retailer, a retail developer, or investor will tell you what is most important to them. Note that because different retailers place emphasis on different things, the following is only a general list of the requirements of retailers:

- Location of their customers
- Convenience—easy in and out (ingress and egress), on the best side of the road, depending on the business
- Visibility—can the shop(s) be easily seen in enough time to turn in?
- Other tenants in the same area—will their customers be my customers?
- Competition—some is good, but too much is bad (see the example following this list)
- Taxing jurisdiction
- City or county boundaries
- Local laws and ordinances that might affect sales or store operations
- Traffic patterns and stoplights
- am or pm side of road

How much competition is good?

Years ago, we saw the birth of the home improvements store. They started one of the first new **big boxes** as a conversion of their contractor model into a more user-friendly consumer model. Depending on where you lived, you might have seen HQ (Home Quarters), Hechinger's, Home Depot, Lowe's, or Scotty's. Some of these retailers may still supply contractors, but they must have a certain number of rooftops—homes—within their trade area to be profitable (their trade area depends on other choices the shopper has nearby). One home improvement store can satisfy a market, and two might be able to generate enough business in one trade area; add a third store and the available dollars to be spent for home improvements is getting pretty thin. The first one to open captures the market; the second defines it; and the third may oversaturate it. We've seen the same trend with electronics stores and sporting goods big boxes.

Just having enough rooftops is not the answer. What is needed are the right rooftops and residents who want and will patronize your type of development. Here's an example of a land deal that overlooked these considerations.

A developer had an idea to bring a popular but new-to-the-area grocery store into an up-and-coming bedroom community in a nearby city. The site was zoned for business, and its configuration supported a nice layout and good traffic flow. Based on the site plan, the economics looked good, and the developer struck a preliminary deal with the grocery chain.

At a meeting with the zoning administrator, the developer learned that the county was dry—that is, no alcohol sales were allowed in the county. The upscale, new-to-the-area grocery store was very proud of its two aisles of beer selection and its large wine department. The lack of alcohol sales was a true deal-breaker for the grocery, and they backed out. It was difficult to find a new user for the site, and the developer ended up selling it to a Walmart Supercenter open 24/7. The neighbors protested, and the protest developed into a protracted lawsuit between the Walmart and the neighbors. The county officials were pulled into it and were very sorry that the county was dry.

After two years of controversy, the Walmart was finally approved, and the voters of the county passed a referendum allowing beer, wine, alcohol, and liquor by the drink to be sold throughout the county.

Types of Retail

Freestanding retail. This could be a grocery store, home improvement store, Walmart, Target, or even a drugstore. These retailers are referred to as *destination-oriented* because they don't depend on traffic brought in by other retailers. The retailers will tell you the information they will need to determine whether or not a site is suitable for their business. These retailers may also serve as anchor tenants for neighborhood or community centers. Also, they may choose to locate with other large tenants in a **power center**, which has multiple large tenants and few, if any, small local tenants.

Demographic reports are important to these tenants, and these tenants have demographic criteria they use to select locations. Some tenants outline their requirements on their websites. They might need to know the number of people living nearby, their incomes, ages, races, occupations, and so on (see Demographics on the following page).

Neighborhood shopping center. **Neighborhood shopping centers** can range in size from 60,000 to more than 200,000 square feet. Their trade area ranges from one to three to five miles depending on where their competition is located. They are typically anchored by a grocery store and other retail uses needed on a daily or weekly basis by the surrounding residents.

Community shopping center. Larger than neighborhood shopping centers, **community shopping centers** are 250,000 to 500,000 square feet. They have multiple anchor tenants and have a larger trade area. Depending on who the big tenants are, where their other locations are, and where their competition is located, the trade area might be as much as 10 miles or more. A neighborhood center may be part of the community center.

Regional centers, open malls, and enclosed malls. At 500,000 square feet and up, many **regional centers** cover more than 1 million square feet and have extensive trade areas depending on their department stores. A mall can have a trade area of 100 miles or more. In many ways, a mall development is like a small city and should be treated differently than other types of retail. While demographic reports are still key for them, mall developers and small tenants will look at a much larger trade area because of the mall size and the fact that some are totally enclosed.

Demographics

Retailers and retail developers typically use some type of demographic information when making decisions. These reports can be compiled by individuals but are more commonly done by third-party companies specializing in data collection and reporting. Doing the data compilation yourself can be daunting because you must use the raw census tracts and extract the information you need. Companies who do this are able to format the data as specified and provide the information you need quickly. Also, if you are marketing a property, unbiased, third-party data—that from a recognized demographics company—has more credibility than data you compiled to market your property. Look online to find demographic report providers. The CCIM offers demographic information to its candidates and designees as a membership benefit.

Demographic reports use the census data, perhaps add other research, and then estimate the numbers for the current year (because the census is taken only every 10 years). Some of the data categories you'll find are the following:

- Population
- Age
- Race
- Income by household and per capita
- Number and ages of children
- Drive time to work
- Education level

When they require information about an area, tenants or developers can order a report, specify the categories desired, and choose their preferred area (usually stated in radius miles). For example, a grocer might order a report for a one-, three-, and five-mile ring around the site they are considering to see if those living nearby are their type of customers. How would they know? The grocers know the type of customer they appeal to—by age, education, income, et cetera. Note that not all demographic studies are performed in a ring; some have their boundaries drawn to truly represent their trade area.

Example

There are hundreds of workers who drive from the suburbs into the central business district every day. They drive north on Hwy. 1 and the speed limit is 50 miles per hour. Most enter Hwy. 1 from State Street from the east where the speed limit is 45 miles per hour.

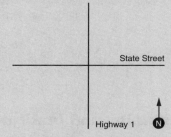

State Street

Highway 1   N

All other things being equal, where do you think a Starbucks would prefer to be located?

   a.   On the SE corner of State and Hwy. 1

   b.   On the SW corner of State and Hwy. 1

   c.   On the NW corner of State and Hwy. 1

   d.   On the NE corner of State and Hwy. 1

   e.   On any of the four corners

   f.   On any location on Hwy. 1

   g.   On any location on State Street

Think about what Starbucks sells (coffee products), when the most popular time to buy them would be (in the morning), where the customers would be coming from (east and south), and what would determine whether or not they would stop there (convenience). Which corner is most convenient?

The best answer is (d), the NE corner. This location allows for a right turn in and a right turn out and is on the "away from home" or "going to work" side of the street.

Let's do the same exercise with the same roads and conditions, but let's use a grocery store. Also assume that many of the workers drive in the same pattern as described in the example above.

Where is the best location for the grocery?

   a.   On the SE corner of State and Hwy. 1

   b.   On the SW corner of State and Hwy. 1

   c.   On the NW corner of State and Hwy. 1

   d.   On the NE corner of State and Hwy. 1

   e.   On any of the four corners

   f.   On any location on Hwy. 1

   g.   On any location on State Street

Do people buy groceries on the way to work or on the way home? Do they try to buy groceries closer or farther away from home?

The best answer is (a), the SE corner, though (g), any location on State Street, may be a good location if it is a long drive home from the intersection. In this situation, a grocery store would typically want to be on the "going toward home" side of the street and be no farther away from home than it takes for frozen food to start to defrost.

Don't worry about having to do this analysis for all retailers. Many will have done it themselves and will tell you in detail what their needs are. The point is that much of this is common sense.

■ Industrial, Multifamily, and Institutional-Use Properties

Industrial, multifamily, and institutional-use properties are routinely handled by industry specialists. Larger developments may be purchased by institutional investors, such as **pension funds**, life insurance companies, and **real estate investment trusts (REITs)**. It is unlikely that a beginning commercial broker will be involved in properties such as these except to handle a lease for a small commercial industrial property or a small apartment building.

Industrial Developments

Industrial developments have very different needs depending on what type of industrial use it is—manufacturing or warehousing—and where they need to be located—near an airport, an interstate highway, or in a special district like a foreign trade zone. Talk with the economic development department in your area for an explanation of incentives such as **foreign trade zones (FTZs)**. In an FTZ, a manufacturer may be able to defer tariffs on imported parts until fabrication is partially or fully complete. This deferral of expense helps with a business's cash flow.

Industrial developers may be building for one or more large users or for multiple smaller users. The business may be manufacturing, warehousing, combinations of these, and office. Industrial properties are handled by industrial specialists who know the market and the trends and particularly the needs of industrial users. When selling developed properties, the tenant may be a good prospect.

Some of the things important to industrial users are location in an FTZ (or other area with tax incentives); proximity to the airport or intermodal facility (where different methods of transportation meet, such as air, rail, roads, and ports); proximity to major highways; availability of utilities at the capacity needed; proximity to workforce; proximity to rail; taxing jurisdiction; municipality; building design (floor loads, ceiling heights); and ingress and egress.

Multifamily Properties

Multifamily properties, or apartment complexes, are sold as investment properties. It is highly unlikely that a typical investment group would reside in one or more of the units. Institutional investors look for apartment properties of a certain size—usually over 200 units—and quality. Further, these investors look for locations in urban areas, but will consider properties in smaller towns, if the employment levels and economics justify the investment. Smaller apartment buildings are also brokered by commercial agents but are outside the scope of this book.

In the list below are some of the things a typical renter might seek (remember that we are dealing with location and site issues, not apartment features). If a property is attractive to a renter, it is attractive to an investor.

- Reasonable topography
- Attractive landscaping with trees and other natural features
- Visibility to major roads
- Proximity to amenities (shopping, restaurants, houses of worship)
- Good access
- Convenience to places of employment
- Public transportation (depends on the market)
- Jurisdiction—city, county
- School district
- Taxing district
- Voting district
- Nearby properties or land features
- Where the competition is located
- Traffic congestion

There are certainly more considerations, but those listed will give commercial real estate practitioners an idea of the differences in land use and desirability. When working with multifamily properties, we have stepped into another arena and must consider different things because this is where people live, not work. Now the concerns focus on the nonwork hours, where the previous uses focused on the work hours.

An investor will make an investment decision based primarily on the cash return of the property. The cash return will be dependent on the property's income (occupancy and rental rate are the keys here) and the property's expenses.

Special-Use Properties

Some developers have unique specialties that have their own specific site requirements. Let's look at a few below.

Churches.   A church development is typically started by the church's congregation. They may have a site or go to a developer for a site. What are they looking for? Churches can be among the most difficult clients because the members of the church, mosque, or synagogue are volunteers, not land-use experts or architects. Still, they may have strong opinions about how the development should proceed.

Generally what these people need is a location convenient to their present and future congregation, enough land to expand, compatible neighbors, and easy access.

Government buildings and public structures.   Depending on use, the requirements for this type of development will be those found in the office section above, with the addition of community revitalization. Sometimes public buildings will be built in an area needing revitalization, and the government is the first to start the redevelopment process. The government agencies may have traded for the land or be using land that was in their inventory. Their site selection may have nothing to do with highest and best use for the intended use.

Hotel sites.   Again, developing hotel sites depends on the product. Is this a budget facility, a midprice hotel with services, a four-star, full-service luxury hotel, an extended-stay hotel, or an interstate-interchange motel? Does the hotel cater to business travelers or vacation travelers? Is it budget, luxury, or somewhere between? Is the site meant for a single building or for a resort with a golf course and other amenities? Is the owner a franchise or independent?

The hotel and hospitality business is very specialized. The operators will tell the broker of their exact needs and requirements for their sites. Factors like visibility and access will always be important, and there will be other specifics that may pertain only to a hospitality product.

Land

Many brokers are involved in the sale of land. After all, it all begins with the land. Land brokerage is a specialty that will be covered in detail later in this book. There are many details to know when assisting a buyer or seller with the sale of land (see Chapter 4).

■ Summary

We have looked at many property types. What we have not covered yet are the internal aspects of commercial real estate, such as financing, marketing, creating pro formas, writing contracts, leasing, and managing the property.

Each type of commercial real estate has characteristics that set it apart from the others. A good commercial broker will know and understand these characteristics before undertaking any involvement. There is much more to learn about each one. Read industry publications, browse the internet, and check organizations mentioned in Chapter 1 for details.

case study	**Office Users**

Think about what you have learned about office users and what is important to them. Based on the following descriptions, determine the three most important things for that office user.

1. Insurance office of 2,000 square feet; three employees who work out of the office; clients come to their office.

   _____

   _____

   _____

2. Doctor's clinic of 5,000 square feet; family practice; does some out-patient procedures.

   _____

   _____

   _____

3. Headquarters location for a multibillion-dollar international bank; estimate 600,000 square feet for this location; employs thousands of people and has several regional offices.

_____

_____

_____

4. Credit card processing facility of 250,000 square feet; open 24/7 but not open to the public.

_____

_____

_____

■ Review Questions

1. Demographics would most likely be *MOST* important to which type of user?
   a. Office
   b. Retail
   c. Multifamily
   d. Hotel

2. Visibility would be *LEAST* important to which type of user?
   a. Grocery store
   b. Drugstore
   c. Credit card processing facility
   d. Insurance agency

3. A foreign trade zone (FTZ) would appeal *MOST* to which type of user?
   a. Industrial
   b. Shopping center
   c. Office building
   d. Church

4. A five-story office building would *MOST* likely be classified as
   a. single tenant.
   b. lowrise.
   c. midrise.
   d. highrise.

5. A bagel shop would *MOST* likely choose which location?
   a. "Going toward home" side of the street
   b. "Going to work" side of the street
   c. Left turn in, left turn out
   d. Any of these

3

Investors and Other Types of Buyers

overview

Whether you plan to work with buyers or sellers of commercial real estate, you must understand the thought processes of investors, who may be your primary clients. By understanding what they are looking for, you will be in a better position to meet your clients' property needs or market your sellers' properties effectively. ■

learning objectives

When you have completed this chapter, you will be able to

■ describe different types of investors,

■ list how to qualify buyers,

■ explain the difference between users and investors, and

■ describe the basics of a 1031 exchange.

■ Key Terms

build to suit	institutional investor	safe harbor
capital gains	joint venture	sale-leaseback
end user	qualified intermediary (QI)	

■ Types of Investors

The following are different types and levels of investment buyers:

- The individual investor, usually seeking lower-priced to midpriced properties
- The joint venture and partnership, usually seeking midpriced to higher-priced properties
- The institutional investor, usually seeking higher-priced properties

Let's start with the individual investor. While there are many types of individual investors, we will focus on those seeking investment properties in the $500,000 to $2 million range. With this investor, it is especially important to qualify needs (using the list in this chapter) so the right property can be located. Depending on the market, quality properties in this price range may be limited. The best bet may be a stand-alone retail space or small building. Residential choices could include duplexes or a very small apartment complex. Again, the broker needs to ascertain how involved in the management the investor wants to be.

The **joint venture** and partnership is usually a midrange investor that may be seeking properties in the $2 million to $5 million range, such as a very small shopping center, an office building, an industrial facility, or a small apartment complex.

The **institutional investor** is usually a higher-range investor that may be seeking properties (or even a portfolio of properties) in the $5 million and higher range. This investor can cover the purchase of any of the properties mentioned above, plus office complexes, medium to large shopping centers, industrial parks, and large apartment complexes. Investors in this category are typically pension funds, life insurance companies, and real estate investment trusts (REITs). They may be represented by a portfolio advisor, fund manager, or asset manager who may work through select investment brokers. Properties considered may not even be officially on the market. It is common for a broker to call owners of desired properties to see if a sale would be considered.

■ Investment Sales

As a broker meeting with a potential investor for the first time, you should ask the following questions and understand answers you receive.

1. "How many other properties do you own?" The answer gives you an idea of how experienced your buyer is.
2. "Why you are looking to buy this property at this time?" This question can open lots of doors. It may be that the investors are anxious to find a 1031 exchange replacement property. Because there is very limited time to identify and close on replacement property, you have been given a timetable. It may be that the investor has been waiting for this property to become available. It may be that their golf buddy just bought something like this, and they want to buy a similar property too.
3. "What are your other real estate holdings?" What kind of returns are you getting on these? Is the investor sticking to one type of property or creating a diversified portfolio? Is there a specific price range the investor feels most comfortable with? What will the investor be comparing everything to?
4. "Is your purchase contingent upon anything other than finding the right property at the right price?" Try to flush out any circumstances beyond your

control. Perhaps the investor is getting divorced, dissolving a partnership, or waiting for another property to close.

5. "Who besides you will participate in the decision-making process?" This question helps determine who the decision maker really is. You always want to be dealing with the decision maker. If you can't, you need to know the decision-making process being followed.

6. "What are the deal specifics?" Find out what the investors want and discover any constraints by asking the following:
   - How much do you plan to invest?
   - How much cash do you have to put down?
   - What types of returns are you seeking over what period of time?
   - How long do you plan to hold the property?
   - What type of property will you consider?
   - What are your deal breakers (those things a buyer just won't agree to, such as certain locations, timing, tenants they don't want, etc.)?
   - Do you have a lender you typically use?
   - Are you in the process of a 1031 exchange? If so, where in the process are you?

7. "Where do you live, and how active will you be in the management of the property?" For example, an investor from New Jersey might enjoy visiting his or her investment property in Virginia Beach more than a property in Lynchburg, Virginia.

8. "What do you want me to do for you?" This question's answer lets you know the investor's expectations. They may want you to only find the properties and then their team will take it from there.

9. "Have you worked with a broker before? Who was it, and how did it go?" The response to this question gives you an idea of whether the investors understand what you can do and gives you some insight into their previous experiences.

10. "What are your long-range investment goals?" This question may have been answered in previous discussions, but you need to know this before you move on. The following are the typical things an investment buyer will consider:
    - Return on the investment
    - Tax benefits
    - Degree of management
    - Appreciation
    - How much they can borrow (referred to as *leverage*)

Investors may calculate return on investment in different ways or by using different assumptions. Typically a return on an investment is the profit in relation to the investment. The following is a simple example:

Dan invests $1,000. Every year he receives a check for $50. His yearly return is 5% (50 ÷ 1,000). At the end of the fifth year, Dan sells his investment and receives his $50 plus his $1,000 back. He invested $1,000 and received $50 every year. Over the period, he received $50 × 5 = $250.

Fred invested $1,000 and also receives $50 per year. However, at the end of five years when he sells, he not only gets his $50 per year but gets $1,200 back. His return for the holding period is higher than Dan's because he received an additional $200 at the end. Over the period, he received $50 × 5 + $200 = $450.

We will look at different ways to determine returns in Chapter 6.

Tax law changes influence the desirability and value of investment real estate. Brokers should ask their investors to explain which tax benefits are important to them. The typical responses are depreciation deductions, expense deductions, tax credits, deferred taxes, and sheltering the investor's other income. Because tax laws change frequently, the best way to find out about what laws currently affect commercial real estate is to talk to your tax expert for a primer on current tax law affecting commercial real estate.

Some properties are more management-intensive than others. Good management may be able to make the difference between a property being profitable or unprofitable. For example, if a property manager practices routine preventative maintenance (such as cleaning or changing air-conditioning filters regularly), that property manager may prevent large repairs. It's just like how you deal with your own car and home. Do you change the oil in your car as recommended? Do you check the air pressure in your tires? How about your home? Do you clean the filters, repair rotted wood, have your air conditioner serviced even though it is working? It's the same for a commercial building. As with homes and cars, some commercial buildings require more maintenance than others.

We used to expect the value of our real estate to increase. Likewise, we expected our commercial real estate investments to increase in value. However, commercial real estate bought solely as an investment may be valued purely on the value of the leases in place, not on the value of the lot and the building. A property can lose value if good quality tenants leave and cannot be replaced. An empty building with no prospects of occupancy (and rent) has diminished value. In some cases, the land may have appreciated and could be sold at a profit. The fundamental value of investment real estate is the value of the income stream and that starts with the rent. In the case of an owner-occupied building, it may be valued as a home is valued rather than on its income stream. However, because the next buyers might not want the property for their business, we need to always look at commercial real estate as if it will be purchased by an investor. If the income continues to rise, then the value most likely will too.

■ IRS 1031 Exchange

In 1990, the Internal Revenue Service (IRS) issued the rules on deferred exchanges. Section 1.1031 of the Internal Revenue Code lays out in detail the procedures for turning a sale-and-purchase transaction into an exchange. If an exchange is done correctly, some or all of the taxable **capital gains** may be deferred. Note that capital gains may be taxed at a lower rate than ordinary income—check with a tax advisor.

The "like kind" provision for real property is quite broad and includes land, rental, and business property, any of which can be exchanged for the other. In general, like-kind real estate is property held for investment or business purposes. The like-kind provision for personal property is more restrictive.

The rules also require that the exchanger use a **safe harbor** to hold the proceeds while the exchange is in progress and spell out what those safe harbors are. One type of safe harbor for exchangers is a **qualified intermediary (QI)**. A QI can be a person or company who does not have ownership or interest in the properties being exchanged, nor represents the exchangers, such as their attorneys.

The rules also require certain time limits and other requirements, the details of which are described in the regulations. Coordinating a 1031 exchange requires a complete understanding of those regulations and requirements. One simple error or missing the deadline by only a day can create serious tax consequences for the exchanger.

Before contemplating a 1031 exchange, a broker must contact an expert in this complex process such as a certified public accountant (CPA), attorney, or a qualified intermediary. However, a broker must understand the advantages of suggesting such a method when a seller is interested in selling property.

A seller may have held property for some time. If the property were to be sold as an outright sale, there may be significant capital gains taxes due. A 1031 exchange may allow the seller to exchange the investment or business property for another investment or business property. Depending on the values of the properties, the seller may be able to defer capital gains taxes until a later date. Of course it will limit any cash proceeds, but if cash isn't needed and tax concerns are paramount, then a 1031 exchange should be considered.

Commercial brokers should have a basic understanding of the requirements of the 1031 regulations as well as the risks and benefits of the 1031 exchange so they can better advise their clients. Extensive information is available online. Tax laws change, so check with your tax professional or the IRS for current rules.

■ Owner-Occupied Properties and Build to Suit

Users of office and industrial space will contract with owners and developers to build a building to meet their specifications—**build to suit** their needs. The end user may either buy the building or lease it on a long-term lease. In the case of a sale, the developer may not care about design or size of the building unless the building is part of a larger development. However, in the case of a lease, the developer needs to be aware of anything that would make the building unmarketable or undesirable to other users in the event that the tenant moves out early. It takes time to recoup funds on a development, and should the lease not be honored, the owners may find themselves owners of a white elephant—an empty building.

Sale-Leaseback

An alternative to buying outright is to engage in a **sale-leaseback**. The first step in a sale-leaseback is to call on the owners to see if they are interested in selling their property. They tell you that they could use the money from the sale in order to upgrade their equipment, but they want to keep their business operation where it is. How would you market that?

Well, it depends on how strong those owners would be as tenants. Remember that when selling leased property, unless the owners intend to redevelop the site or re-tenant the building, it's the credit of the tenants (or potential tenants) plus the terms of the lease that creates the value.

How strong is the business of the owners? What does their balance sheet look like? How much longer do they intend to stay in business and stay there? Do they need the cash to keep the business afloat?

If the business of the owners looks strong, this type of property can be marketed as an investment. It can be directly marketed to investors you know or through brokers who represent investors. Perhaps this would be a good investment for you!

The owners will need to be willing to open their books to potential buyers and to sign a long-term lease. If the business of the owners is a public company, the owners should have audited financial records. The owners need to have their attorney and CPA involved to ensure that their interests are addressed.

Keep in mind that no matter how strong a business appears to be, a downturn in the market, a change in environmental regulations, or a change in the tax law can cause a business to close its doors. If you plan to invest in single-owner buildings, be sure to consider the risks should the tenant leave.

■ Other Buyer Types

Perhaps one of your early transactions will be with the buyer who is the **end user**. In other words, the buyer is buying it for his or her own use. It might be an office user (insurance agent, appraiser, architect, doctor, government agency, etc.). While everyone wants to buy wisely, the buyer may have considerations other than investment when buying.

When working with a buyer who plans to use the space for his or her business, ask questions about the business itself. What size facility is needed? What zoning is required? Where do the customers frequenting the business work or live? Where do the employees of the business live? Where does the buyer live?

You will need to qualify the buyer as you would qualify a tenant in the building— what are his or her needs? You will also need to qualify the buyer as you would an investor, using the questions listed earlier in this chapter. You see, this buyer is wearing two hats—investor and end user, where the needs of one might override the needs of the other. Your careful questioning and listening will determine what is most important to this buyer.

■ Summary

Understanding buyer types is critical to be successful in commercial real estate. Fortunately, if you can ask questions and listen to the answers, you will have a real advantage over others because they may not be asking the right questions or even listening. In this chapter, we learned about different buyer types and some of the questions to ask.

| case study | **Selling a Shopping Center** |

Stephanie owns a shopping center. She has owned it for several years, and it has increased in value. Many buyers have approached her about selling it. Frankly, they are offering her very attractive prices. She is tempted but doesn't need the money right now. What are her choices?

_____

_____

_____

_____

_____

■ Review Questions

1. A manufacturer needs a building but has unusual needs in the layout and construction of the facility. What would be the best fit for the company?

    a. Sale-leaseback

    b. Build to suit

    c. 1031 exchange

    d. Investment sale

2. The sellers are concerned about how much they will owe in taxes on the profits of their building. What is one way to defer taxes?

    a. Sale-leaseback

    b. Build to suit

    c. 1031 exchange

    d. Sell at the end of the fiscal year

3. Manufacturers need additional money to upgrade their equipment. The only real assets they have are their building and their business. They have a viable business but need to borrow money for the equipment. What might they consider?

    a. Sale-leaseback

    b. A new build to suit

    c. 1031 exchange

    d. Declaration of bankruptcy

4. An investor wants to invest in commercial real estate. He has two children who will be ready for college in three years. The money he wants to invest in the real estate will be needed for college tuition. What would you advise?

    a. Invest in an office building project under development

    b. Consider a more liquid investment, such as CDs or treasuries

    c. Buy an occupied building and lease it back to the tenant

    d. Invest in land

5. An investor is interested in buying as many properties as possible with as little money as possible. This means the loans will be as high as possible. This type of financing is referred to as

    a. high leverage.

    b. mid leverage.

    c. low leverage.

    d. investor grade.

Insider Knowledge

4 Land

overview

It all starts with the land. Even if not selling land, the broker needs a basic understanding of the issues faced in land brokerage because that understanding will be helpful in all other commercial real estate transactions. The land brokers (also referred to as *dirt brokers*) operate quite differently from other types of brokers, and they often have an intimate connection with the land. Because of this, land can be one of the most exciting areas of real estate. ■

learning objectives

When you have completed this chapter, you will be able to

■ describe ownership rights, and

■ list key elements of due diligence.

■ Key Terms

air rights	highest and best use	subsurface rights
building code	lien	surface rights
compaction	life estate	title
deed of trust	mineral rights	topography
deed restrictions	mortgage	unsubordinated
easement	percolation	water rights
encroachment	subordinated	zoning

■ What Is Land?

When most people think about land, they think of the surface rights. When petroleum companies think about land, they think about subsurface or mineral rights. When cellular service companies think about land, they may be thinking of air rights. When utility companies or farmers think about land that adjoins a river or other body of water, they may be thinking about water rights.

So what is land? The following are some of the rights constituting the reality of land (see Figure 4.1):

- **Surface rights** include the right to construct a building or a parking lot, plant crops, and, in general, to use the top part (surface) of the land.
- **Subsurface rights** cover the right to mine for minerals, extract elements, and run piping or optic fiber—in other words, the right to do things underground.
- **Air rights** are the right to use the space above the land or a building. This includes cell towers on top of buildings or buildings on top of other buildings.
- **Water rights** cover the limited right to use water bordering on or running through a property for irrigation or recreation.

Figure 4.1 | Land Rights

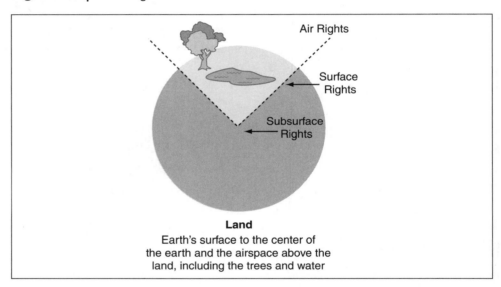

Land
Earth's surface to the center of
the earth and the airspace above the
land, including the trees and water

The Benefits of the Bundle of Rights

When selling land, sellers can only convey what they have. In other words, if sellers (or previous sellers) have sold the **mineral rights** of a property to a coal mining company, then whoever buys that property does not receive the mineral rights to that property in their "bundle of rights." In certain parts of the country, it is not uncommon for all of the mineral rights to have been sold, so that only the surface and air rights (and maybe water rights) remain. It is important for dirt brokers to check the title documents to see exactly what is being conveyed and what is not.

An owner of a land's mineral rights probably has some limited surface rights to allow them to access the subsurface. It may be in the form of an easement—the right to use someone else's property for a stated purpose in a stated area. This stated purpose is important to ascertain because the easement holder's rights may interfere with what a buyer wishes to do with the property. We'll learn more about easements later in this chapter.

Let's look at another example of land rights that can be purchased. As stated above, air rights refer to the right to use the space over another's property. What value might there be in air rights? The following are some examples of air-right value:

- In cities where high density is common and developers need to build up, not out, the air rights may be worth more than the surface rights.
- Cellular phone companies want some towers high up and would prefer to place towers atop a building.
- A phase II (expansion) of an office building with a different ownership structure might be best located on top of the existing phase I building (of course, this assumes the foundation of the phase I building can handle the extra load).
- A hotel may be best located atop a convention center or a trade market in a vibrant central business district.
- A condominium project may be well suited atop a downtown parking garage.
- A developer may have a perfect project to go over a railway.

We can think of many ways to use air rights (see Figure 4.2). As land becomes scarcer, air rights will become more valuable. From the examples of air and mineral rights, you can see the importance of paying attention to all of the rights that come with a piece of land, rather than just the surface rights.

Figure 4.2 | Air Rights

■ Types of Development

Even if we know what rights we can buy for a given tract of land, we still have much to learn about the tract. For instance, what about the location? When we speak of a great location, we need to qualify our statement by asking, "great for what?" Some tracts of land would be good for many types of development, but there are always one or two uses that are superior to the others. This brings us to the concept of the highest and best use of a piece of land.

Highest and best use means the use that is legally permissible, economically feasible, and that will produce the highest return to the owner. So, let's say we have a 20-acre parcel zoned for four dwellings per acre. We'll give the name R4 to this zoning classification. Let's say there is a need for apartments, and, if we could build 18 units per acre—let's call it RMF18—we could sell the parcel for $1.5 million. So is the highest and best use RMF18? Well, is rezoning to RMF18 feasible? If rezonable, then maybe apartments are the highest and best use; if not, then no. Wishing doesn't count in highest and best use.

When evaluating highest and best use for a piece of land, you can use the characteristics best suited to each type that we discussed in Chapter 2. The following is a brief look at the different types of development and key characteristics required for highest and best use:

- *Retail.* The key characteristics required are demographics, demographics, demographics, and next are visibility, access, and competition.
- *Office.* The key characteristics are location of the labor pool, location of the executives' homes, and location of the business's supplies and customers.
- *Industrial.* The key characteristics are access to highways, airports, sea ports, and rail lines; soil conditions; economic incentives; and proximity to the labor pool.
- *Multifamily.* For our purposes, let's narrow this to investment-grade apartment complexes of 200 units or more. The key characteristics are convenience to places of employment, school districts, amenities, and transportation.
- *Special-purpose developments.* Houses of worship, government buildings, and hotels have their key characteristics. Ask the buyers or users what is most important to them.

■ Selling or Leasing Land

"How much is my land worth?" How many real estate agents have been asked that question? As all of them know: It depends. Depends on what?

Selling Land

The following is a look at the questions an agent would need to answer in order to be able to advise a buyer or seller on the value of a tract of land:

- Where is it (this begins to address the location issue)?
  - Is there new development nearby?
  - Are there new roads being built?
  - Are water and sewers being brought into the area?
  - Is there a new employer coming into the area?
  - Is there a large employer leaving the area?
  - Is this some place people want to be?
- What are the site characteristics?
  - What is the size of the site?
  - What kind of access to the site is there?
  - How much visibility does the site have?
  - What is the site's topography?
  - How much of the land is usable?

- What are some of the legal, title, and environmental issues?
    - Are there any encroachments?
    - What's its zoning?
    - Are there any protected species, historical issues, or development constraints?
    - Does any part of the site sit in a floodplain? Is any part of the site classified as wetlands?
    - What is the quality of the title?
    - Which jurisdiction is it in?
    - What are the soil conditions?
    - Are utilities available and, if so, in what capacity? If not, what is the cost to bring them to the site?
    - Have any rights been sold? In other words, which ownership rights will pass with the title?
    - Are there any environmental issues known?
- Are there any market issues?
    - How much other, similar land is there nearby? Are there plenty of other sites or is this the only game in town?
    - Who is next door? How is their property being used?
    - What does your area look like?
    - What do people have to drive through to get to this site?
    - Can the property be easily rezoned? If so, to what can it be rezoned?

This list of questions could go on and on, depending on where the tract is, how large it is, and so on.

Land is valued in two ways—the market approach and the income approach. The most common method used is the market approach. We will discuss the income approach later in Chapter 6. To determine value using either approach, the agent must answer the questions above to determine the usability, desirability, and marketability of the property.

Let's say an agent has gathered enough information to start developing a comparative market analysis (CMA). To value property using the market approach, the agent should compare the subject property to comparable properties that have sold recently. By comparing the recent "solds," the agent can estimate what price the subject property should bring in an open and competitive market, free of unusual influence.

Leasing Land

For a variety of reasons, land may be leased rather than sold. From the seller's side, the reasons for leasing may include the following:

- *Avoidance of capital gains tax.* Although the capital gains rate on long-term investments has dropped substantially over the past few years, many landowners would prefer to defer or avoid paying taxes on their land's appreciation. Instead, they may prefer to offer a long-term land lease and pay taxes (if not sheltered elsewhere) on the lease income.
- *Title issues.* There may be restrictions from passing title outside the family or other ownership group. Some property may be held in such a way that a fee simple sale is not possible.

■ *Desire to retain land.* Some landowners have a belief that they should never sell their property. They are willing to let others use it but are not willing to transfer title.

■ *Pride of ownership.* Some landowners want to be part of the development ownership, and by contributing the land via lease, they can participate in the development yet retain control of their land.

■ *Owned by the government.* The land could be owned by the local, state, or federal government.

From the buyers' side, they may prefer leasing rather than buying for one major reason: There is less up-front cost, depending on interest rates and terms. The following is an example:

Assume:

■ Land value = $1 million.

■ Construction interest rate is 5%.

■ Construction period is 12 months (short period).

■ Interest carry on the land only is more than $50,000 ($1 million × 5% = $50,000), and while that interest is not compounded, the construction interest will be.

Therefore, in the first 12 months, the developer will need $50,000 to carry the land and then $1 million to pay for the land.

If the land is then financed in the mortgage loan, the interest rate will make a big difference in determining which way is the best way to go. Remember that very few commercial developments receive higher than 75% to 80% loan-to-value financing. Using the 75% rate means that the developer would need to have $250,000 of the land covered in cash (equity).

If the land were to be leased, the landowner might allow a lower rate during construction and there would be no interest carry (just lease payments) and no cash needed toward the land.

It all gets down to what a developer can finance versus what terms a landowner will offer. The landowner requires 15% of the property value as rent: $1 million × 15% = $150,000/year. The developer, on the other hand, can purchase the property and finance 80% for 20 years at 5% = $63,355/year but would need $200,000 cash to put down.

Land leases for developments are typically for a long term—40 years or more plus options to renew, but some of the smaller developments, say a restaurant, may be for a shorter period. At the end of the lease, the land and improvements revert to the landowner. The developers must ensure that they received all profit before the lease is ended.

Land leases may be **subordinated** or **unsubordinated**. From the developer's point of view, subordinated is desirable. A subordinated ground lease means that the landowner will take a secondary position to another, typically a lender. When a lender makes a real estate loan, the lender wants to be in the "first" position when it comes to claims on title. Then if the loan becomes delinquent or goes into default, the lender is first to get their money back. With a subordinated lease, the landowners (who are first in line by right) agree to let the lender stand in front of them, thus making the loan more attractive to a lender.

From the landowner's point of view, why give up first position? Depending on the strength of the developer and the developer's tenant(s), the subordination issue may not be a sticking point with a lender. Remember, the lender is trying to minimize risk and ensure that the loan will be repaid. If the tenant is well capitalized, such as Walmart, then the lender is less worried that the property might have to be sold in a foreclosure sale. If the tenant is not a strong one and the owners agree to subordinate their interest, they may lose rights to their land in the case of a foreclosure.

■ Legal Issues with Land

While you are not expected to be a land attorney, every agent should be aware of potential legal issues that could arise and cause problems for your buyer or seller. Discussed below are some of the basics.

Estates in Land

In addition to determining which land rights are being conveyed, we must also look at what type of ownership interest is offered. Typically land is conveyed "fee simple." *Fee* means that the ownership is inheritable; that is, it can be passed down to an owner's heirs. There are complicated variations on this, and an experienced real estate attorney should be consulted if there are any questions as to the type or quality of title.

Another type of estate is a **life estate**. That means the owners of the life estate owns it during their life. Once their life is over, so is their ownership. For example, let's say that Mrs. Brown has a life estate interest in a tract of land. That means that she owns it until her life ends. This is not a fee estate because her ownership ends when she dies. It is not an inheritable estate. She can sell or lease it, but remember that whoever buys it buys what she has to give—ownership during her lifetime. That means if Mr. Smith buys it he will own it as long as Mrs. Brown is alive. When she dies, so does Mr. Smith's ownership. So, you say, why would anyone buy a life estate? How would it be valued?

Given the example above, you can see why life estates may be heavily discounted because of their finite but uncertain time frame. Another type of life estate is a "pur autre vie." It means "for the life of another." We will not discuss this type of estate. If you encounter one of these, consult your attorney.

Let's look at a practical example of a commercial real estate transaction involving a life estate. This is a case that actually happened in a southern city.

A developer wanted to buy a shopping center and some adjoining land with plans to renovate and expand the center (see Figure 4.3). Because of the unusual site configuration (the site was shallow) a particular tenant's store could not be placed on the existing land and meet zoning and building code requirements.

Figure 4.3 | Shopping Center Site

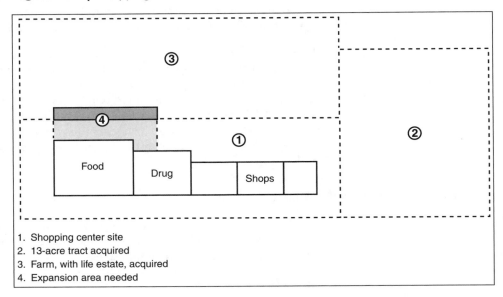

1. Shopping center site
2. 13-acre tract acquired
3. Farm, with life estate, acquired
4. Expansion area needed

There was some land behind the property that could be used to deepen the site. The owner was agreeable to selling the land (while it had been a horse farm, the owner no longer used it for that purpose) but wanted to sell the entire tract rather than just the sliver the developer initially wanted.

The developer was amenable to buying the entire tract, but the owner had another consideration—his elderly mother. She was living in the farmhouse on the property and had been living there for more than 40 years. She was getting old and feeble, and the owner loathed moving her out of her home. He felt that before long she would need to go into a nursing home, but she was not ready to move yet, neither physically nor emotionally (anyone with elderly parents understands this situation).

The owner agreed to sell the land, but only if his mother could retain a life estate in the farmhouse and a small amount of surrounding acreage. The developer could easily carve out the house and some acreage and still be able to develop the center as planned. Eventually the entire tract would be available, and, at that time, the developer could further expand the center or sell off the tract.

What if the developer needed the piece where the mother's house sat? What if the developer assumed that the mother would pass away soon and made development plans based on that? This is an example of thinking ahead and making conservative plans.

Titles

We've looked at the rights being conveyed (or not) and the ownership interest. Let's look at another important factor related to the ownership of land—legal or equitable **title**. The type and quality of title affect the value of the property. In addition, the quality of title impacts the type of financing available, thus having an important impact on the desirability of the land. Having legal title to real estate is the ownership interest held by a lender under a **deed of trust** or a seller with the property under a sales contract. The holder of equitable title means that holder has the right to claim legal title at some point or after a stated event.

For example, a typical owner selling a tract of land that is not financed probably has full title to the property. Once it goes under contract, the buyer has equitable title and the seller still has legal title. The buyer has the right at some point (i.e., closing) to obtain full title.

Another example is the title an owner holds with financed property under a deed of trust. The lender holds legal title through the financing documents and the owner has equitable title—in other words the owner can claim full title once he or she pays off the loan, which he or she has the right to do.

Some states are title theory states and use as their mortgage instrument a deed of trust; other states are lien theory states and use a **mortgage** as their mortgage document. In lien theory states, the owner has title and the lender has a lien against the property.

Deed Restrictions

Any piece of property may be subject to **deed restrictions**. These restrictions are placed on the property by current or previous owners. We are most familiar with restrictive covenants found in many residential neighborhoods. These are a form of deed restrictions. There can be individual restrictions on a property such as prohibiting it from being subdivided, prohibiting sales of alcohol or other products, specifying size or style of the building, and so on.

Common Encumbrances

Just like air rights, subsurface rights and the like are benefits to ownership of land, but there are also items that burden the land. They are called *encumbrances*. While all encumbrances may not prevent title from passing from one party to another, they may affect the value. The most common encumbrances are easements and liens.

Easements. An **easement** is the right to use someone else's property for a stated purpose. There may or may not be a payment involved. These are considered encumbrances on a property; they are a charge against the title (see Figure 4.4).

Figure 4.4 | Easements

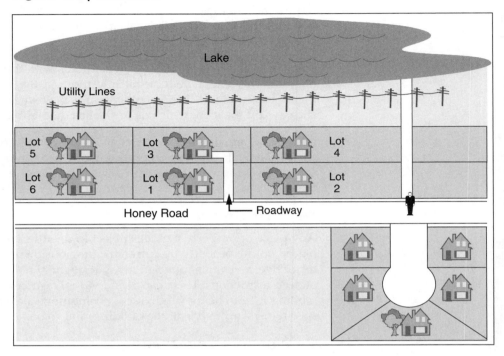

There are many types of easements, and they play an important role in land development. It is important to have any easement in writing and recorded—the more specific, the better. Although the courts may recognize some easements that are not in writing or recorded, these can create title problems, confusion, and delays. Let's look at some common examples of easements below.

Utility easements.   *Utility easements* are rights given by a landowner to the electric, water, sewer, cable television, telephone, and natural gas companies to allow them to come onto or across the land to provide utilities to the site or surrounding sites.

An owner can provide a specific easement—where the exact location of the utility company's lines are specified by a legal description or a blanket easement that gives the utility company the right to use any of the property to accomplish its goal. Which is best for the landowner? Which is best for the utility company?

The answers to these questions are obvious. The landowner wants the necessary utilities but wants them placed on the least desirable part of the land and using the smallest amount of land possible. The owner wants the utility company to be specific about where the lines will go and where the utility company can access the site. The utility company wants as much flexibility as possible so it can provide services at the least cost. It may be cheaper to run overhead power lines across the front and down the middle of the site, but that may detract from the property's value and use. The utility company would prefer a blanket easement.

Access easements.   There are different types, but the purpose of an *access easement* is to provide access to the site or to another site.

For example, consider a plot of six lots (see Figure 4.5). Three of the lots front the street, and three are behind the front three. Without access, the back three lots may be worthless. The owner of all six may want to put in public or private roads for access or may prefer to use an easement through the front lot(s) for access to the rear lots.

Figure 4.5 | Access

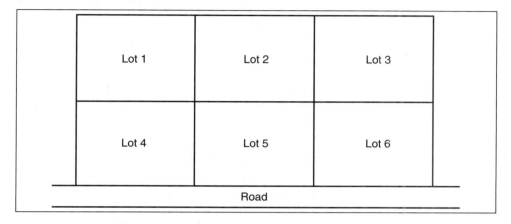

Building code and local ordinances will dictate the minimum criteria for access to a site, so an access easement may not be allowed for certain developable lots. A public or private road may be required.

Further, certain uses may be allowed on lots that have access through an easement, but other uses may require a different kind of access.

For example, on the six lots discussed above, local ordinances may allow homes on lots accessible by easement only but not allow commercial development on them. If they were zoned to allow both residential and commercial uses, the value of the lots would be dictated by how they could be used, that is, their highest and best use. The lots may be worth $20,000 each for residential use but $50,000 each for commercial use. Then let's sell them as commercial lots!

Well, if the local ordinances require exclusive easements, wider easements than provided, or public roads, it is possible that these lots cannot be used for anything other than residential development unless some money is spent to upgrade the access. Further, it may or may not be possible to upgrade the access. If upgrading the access is possible, the cost of doing so may be prohibitive.

Yes, location, location, location is the most important consideration in real estate, but without access, access, access, the value of real estate, if any, is severely impacted.

Personal easements. By definition, *personal easements* allow someone to use another's property for a specific reason. For example, in Charleston, South Carolina, there was a piece of property with a personal easement held by an old Charleston family. The stated purpose of the easement was to allow access to a relative's gravesite. Throughout the years, members of this family tended the grave of a soldier from the Civil War. They had the right in perpetuity (forever) to cross the property of another to access this grave.

Right-of-way easements. The department of transportation may require land for a road right-of-way from a landowner to build or expand access roads. Depending on the circumstances, a fee may or may not be part of the deal.

Building easements.   Depending on local ordinances, certain requirements must be met when constructing improvements on land. In particular, the construction must take place within a building envelope, allowing for space in front (setback), in the back (rear yard), and on the sides (side yards). The amount of space may be dependent on local ordinances, the use, the size, the adjacent uses, and the roads. It may be that a development needs a bit of extra space that they do not have. Depending on the laws and circumstances, it may be possible for an adjoining landowner to grant an easement to their neighbor to provide enough space for a building.

Prescriptive easements.   There is always much speculation about rights of others on someone's land. An easement by prescription may be granted to someone by the courts if the court finds that certain criteria, such as the following, have been met:

- The use must be open and notorious.
- The use must be continual and uninterrupted.
- The use must be for a minimum number of years, depending on the state.

Even when the listed criteria are met, the courts may not allow the use to continue. The overall situation will need to be studied. For example, let's say that there are two adjoining farms. They've been in the same families for 100 years. There is a creek that is thought to adjoin both parcels, but in fact, it adjoins only parcel A. For 50-plus years, the owners of parcel B have crossed parcel A to get to the creek, thinking it was their property. The owner of parcel A dies, and when the heirs sell the property, they realize from the survey that parcel B has been "trespassing" for 50-plus years. Parcel B denies this and states that 100 years ago, it was the intent that both parcels would have access to the water. The owners of Parcel A insist that Parcel B quit crossing the property, and they erect a fence to block passage. Parcel B sues in court, asking for a prescriptive easement—the right to continue to use A's property to access the water. The outcome would depend on the state's requirements for a prescriptive easement claim and the actual evidence presented.

Liens.   Another type of encumbrance on a property is a **lien**. A lien is a charge against the property for some unfulfilled contractual obligation—the most common is the repayment of a debt or other obligation.

In the following, we look at the most common liens.

Mortgage or deed of trust.   Property is pledged as security for a loan. If the loan is not repaid as agreed, then the property can be sold to repay the debt. Financing is covered in further detail in Chapter 7.

Broker's lien.   Some states allow a real estate broker to file a lien for unpaid commissions on commercial property.

Tax liens.   If property or income taxes are not paid, a lien can be placed against the property, and if executed, the property can be sold to repay the tax obligation. Procedures differ among states.

Judgment liens.   These are personal liens created by a party filing a lien against another's property as security to repay a debt owned. Proper legal procedure must be followed, but the property may be sold to repay the debt if so directed by the court.

Zoning, Building Codes, Local Ordinances

Now that we've discovered how the property is owned and what kinds of title, rights, and encumbrances are to be conveyed, let's look at some local issues that directly affect the value and use of land. We will start with what we can build, where it sits on the site, and what types of businesses we can operate.

Most areas have some type of zoning. **Zoning** is local and is unique to the town, city, or county. Zoning dictates land use, location of the buildings on the site, access, and density, among other things. Zoning can be very specific or very general. It depends on how the city or county wants to define how a piece of property can be used.

The initial zoning of an area starts with a plan. The area is broken up into districts that allow specific uses, such as residential, office, retail, industrial, et cetera. There may be many subcategories also, such as single-family (X units to the acre) or multifamily (X units to the acre).

Once an area is initially zoned, a developer wanting to change the classification will need to petition for a rezoning. Again each jurisdiction handles this differently; although, some of the requirements may be similar from area to area. If contemplating a rezoning, it is prudent to attend a rezoning hearing or two to understand the process, time involved, political climate, and general "lay of the land."

Rezoning can hinge on many issues. The following is a typical list of questions concerning events and things to consider:

- What are the surrounding uses?
- Will surrounding uses be adversely impacted by the proposed use?
- What is the planning staff's recommendation?
- Is there an area plan? If so, what does it recommend?
- What is happening in the area?
- What does the economy look like?
- Will this impact the road network, schools?
- Is there adequate police, fire, and emergency protection for the proposed use?
- How does the city, town, or county see itself growing?
- What is desired to be developed in that area?
- Is this development-desired request a political one?
- When are the elections?
- How many jurisdictions have a "say" in the rezoning request?

Besides the use of the land, there are many other components to a rezoning as seen by the following questions:

- Can the land be used for retail?
  - If so, how much retail?
- Are drive-through windows allowed?
  - How many drive-through windows can there be on that site?
- Is there any size limitation on any one tenant?
- How many detached buildings can there be?
- How close to the street can it be?
- Are there requirements for sidewalks, streetlights?

- Must land be reserved for schools, parks, public space, or open space? If so, where and how much?
- How high can the buildings be?

The list of questions goes on and on. Depending on the requirements, many more avenues may need to be explored.

What makes zoning so challenging is that it is determined by local ordinance. Each area (city and county) may have totally different classifications or definitions. For example, B-1, which may be a business classification in some areas, does not mean the same thing in different jurisdictions. Also, rezoning a property may be costly and extremely time-consuming. After much work and money, the rezoning may even be denied.

In addition, local officials may interpret their ordinances differently. Depending on the jurisdiction, the zoning ordinance may be fairly simple or quite complex. It may be amended regularly or seldom. On complicated developments, an owner may need to hire a land-use expert or rezoning expert to help the owner navigate the rules.

Let's suppose that an owner has a large tract of property zoned for residential use. Because of the change in development patterns, this site now seems to be a good site for an office park. Let's say the office zoning category desired is called O-1. It will most likely dictate types of office uses, parking requirements, setbacks, height limitations, size of building, et cetera. In addition to the O-1 requirements, there may be other ordinances or plans that place additional requirements on the development. For example, there may be additional requirements, such as those discussed below.

Open space.   The open space requirement requires some natural areas with vegetation to provide relief from the building and parking lots.

Historic preservation.   There may be structures, or even trees, on the site that have historical significance and must be preserved.

Tree ordinances.   These laws protect trees of a certain size and may require a specified number of trees to be planted in specific locations.

Watershed ordinances.   These can be mandated by many jurisdictions. The *watershed* refers to the path water travels after a rain. Watersheds are critical because they affect our drinking water. When it rains, some water is absorbed into the soil and may make it down to the water table. Some of the rainwater may travel across the land—gravity and topography are the determining factors here—until it is absorbed or empties into a body of water, such as a lake, river, or stream. When flowing toward a body of water, whether it is surface water or in the water table, the water picks up impurities from the surface or from the soils and deposits them in the lake, river, or stream.

Consider the quality of the water that flows across a large asphalt shopping center parking lot. While the water is flowing, it is collecting what has been left behind in the parking lot—oil, gasoline, antifreeze, rubber particles from tires, dust from brake pads, and so on. Then the water moves across the landscaped areas picking up herbicides, pesticides, and fertilizers. Nature can purify some of these pollutants through the filtering ability of certain soils. As the rainwater is absorbed, the soil cleans the water so that when it reaches the water table, it is much cleaner than when it started out.

If there is too much to be absorbed, the water can only flow across land and cannot be cleansed. If there is too much *impervious area*—the area where water cannot be absorbed, such as parking lots, roads, rooftops, paved driveways—then the water just picks up more contaminants on its journey. If the water contains too many or too potent pollutants, then the soil cannot fully cleanse the water. If the soil is not the type to cleanse water—too sandy or too much clay—then the water stays polluted and ends up in the streams. Streams and rivers are the sources for our drinking water, and modern scientific water filtration processes can only clean out so much.

Wetlands protection. As discussed in the watershed section above, there are certain soils that are more efficient in cleansing polluted water. The most effective areas have been classified as "wetlands." While these areas may not look wet or may not even be wet during a dry spell, they are areas with specific soils, flora, and fauna that are effective in screening the pollutants from the surface waters.

Wetlands are identified by government agencies, and depending on their size and other factors, wetlands typically cannot be filled in, disturbed, or removed. There may be provisions to provide other areas to serve as wetlands in the event a wetland area must be filled. This is referred to as *mitigation*, and because mitigation can be a lengthy process, extra time must be budgeted in the land-development timetable to deal with it.

Building code. Be careful not to confuse zoning with **building code**. Zoning deals with land use, density, and building placement. Building code deals with methods and materials for construction.

For example, zoning may allow a piece of land to be used for offices, but the building code will dictate construction materials, disability standards, the need for sprinklers, et cetera. Take a house in a transitional area. The area was a residential neighborhood for many years but now is mostly used for offices. One home is being sold to a business for a business use. It has been used as a residence until now but is zoned office. The home is sold, and the business sets up shop only to discover that it cannot get a business license because the house does not meet the requirement for a business operation. Many of the other homes did, but this one doesn't. Zoning alone does not determine use of an existing structure.

Environmental Issues

We already started the discussion on environmental problems when we discussed watersheds and wetlands. Let's look at some other environmental problems that are important to commercial development.

As seen in the following, different areas have different problems:

- The seashore has concerns about dunes, beach erosion, and protected species.
- The mountains need to have their views and vistas preserved and have issues with protected species and erosion. In addition, acid rain is a concern because of its effect on the trees, soils, and water.
- Urban areas worry about air and water quality, tree canopies, and open space.
- Rural areas face the challenge of herbicides, pesticides, fertilizers, and other agricultural pollutants. Well and septic systems are a primary concern.
- All areas struggle with growth management. How much development is too much? What is good development? What is the impact to the environment?

Many laws and regulations influence how we develop land and deal with such things as the following:

- Air-quality degradation
- Water pollution
- Flooding
- Coastal erosion
- Noise
- Wildlife endangerment
- Sea-life extermination
- Estuary contamination
- Contamination cleanup liability
- Asbestos
- Lead-based paint, pipes, and solder
- Formaldehyde
- Urea formaldehyde foam insulation (UFFI)
- Radon
- Electromagnetic fields (EMFs)
- Underground storage tanks (USTs)
- Hazardous-waste storage and disposal
- Well poisoning
- Polychlorinated biphenyls (PCBs)

Laws and regulations address all these problems. Some environmental problems will be more common than others in commercial land development. Check with your engineer to learn which laws and regulations apply in your development.

When buying land, it is necessary to investigate as much as possible—due diligence—so when the inspection period is over, the buyer will know whether or not to proceed.

For example, the buyer might discover that there is a serious contamination problem on the site that would require some kind of cleanup. The cost and time required to deal with the contamination may be such that the buyer will not be able to complete the development as expected or the buyer may not be able to afford the land.

Another example is discovering wetlands on the property. The buyer must see if the development can be done without disturbing the wetlands and, if not, can there be mitigation? If so, what would the cost be? Finding a one-acre wetlands area in a 100-acre parcel may or may not be a problem at all, depending on where it is and the site design. Finding a one-acre wetland area on a 10-acre parcel is another story, even if the development has planned for substantial open space. Again, it would depend on the location of the wetland and the site design.

Something that land developers dread is the discovery of a protected species or plant on the site. Again, the discovery may be of little impact or the site may be rendered undevelopable.

In the case of environmental issues, a developer will want to have a Phase I Environmental Assessment completed. In addition, most lenders will require this assessment before they will commit to a real estate loan. During this assessment, the environmental engineer will search the title to learn of former uses, inspect the site for "red flags" that could indicate an environmental problem. For example, an environmental engineer may discover a pipe protruding from the ground on a piece of undeveloped property. Why would an undeveloped property have a pipe? What is attached to the underground part of the pipe—an underground storage tank perhaps? If so, what is in that tank? What was it used for? What else might be on that site? This is the typical thought process.

If any red flags are discovered while making a physical inspection or searching the ownership history, a Phase II Environmental Assessment Study will be conducted. During the Phase II Environmental Assessment (the test done after it is determined that further investigation and testing is necessary), the soils, water, and/or air may be tested for contamination or pollutants. It may be that protected species, sites, flora, and fauna will be investigated. A report will be generated with the findings and a recommendation for cleanup or mitigation. If so, arrangements will be made for retesting after the recommendations have been completed or after further investigation is done.

In the protruding-pipe example, the inspecting environmental engineer discovered a pipe protruding from the ground. The engineer would put this discovery in the report (probably after ascertaining that it was not just some random piece of pipe stuck into the ground) and then run tests, such as discovering what the pipe is attached to. If it is attached to nothing, then it's probably a fluke, and the report will so note. If it's an underground storage tank (UST), well, looks like we need further information. Testing of the UST's contents and the surrounding soils and any water will indicate if there may be a problem. The tank could be empty and the surrounding area free of any contaminants.

The report would indicate this good news, and it would likely not interfere with the sale. However, if this was supposed to be a raw tract of land, never used, what is the UST doing there? What else might be there? This and other questions are the reasons why is it important to walk as much of the land as possible.

Another red flag would be a cleared area on a tract that was presumed to be virgin land. Why would it be cleared? Who cleared it?

Contamination can come from a variety of obscure sources. There may have been an above-ground oil tank that leaked (dripped oil on the ground) over the years, causing eventually a contamination problem when the oil entered the water table and traveled with the water.

The surrounding uses of land can have serious impact on a development. Suppose a landfill is uphill from your tract. If there are any breaches in the materials protecting the refuse, contaminants can enter the soil and be carried by water to other sites. Properties miles away can be affected.

Properties used solely for agricultural purposes may seem safe, but consider what has been used on that site. Possibly there could be contamination from trash piles, discarded tires, oil and gasoline from farm machinery, herbicides, fertilizers, pesticides, polluted lagoons, or USTs.

Because the environmental laws indicate who is responsible for cleaning up any found problems, prudent buyers will want to learn all they can before committing to a property.

Site Concerns

Maximizing the land use is an important consideration for developers. That does not mean that the most successful sites are covered with buildings and parking lots, but that the site needs to fit the development, and the development needs to fit the site.

Topography.   The term **topography** refers to the nature of the surface of the land, that is, the contour. Sometimes it is best for a site to be flat; sometimes the developer prefers that the site be sloped. Some rolling hills may even be desired. Severe drop-offs and steep grades are seldom welcome. Building on a steep site can increase construction costs dramatically and create some environmental challenges, such as sediment control. Rain during construction is expected in most parts of the country, but heavy rain while building on a steep site can cause the soils to wash out and run down to a stream or river with a negative impact.

When building on previously undeveloped land, the impact of the construction and the finished product must be evaluated, taking us back to the watershed discussion. Will the watershed change because of this development—will the water be redirected? Will the water move downhill faster than before because the land is smoother due to grading, asphalt, et cetera? What influence will all of these changes have on the land that rests between the development and the river or streams—where the water is heading? What influence will this have on the river and streams? Will the water move so quickly that it will overwhelm them? Will erosion occur?

Flooding.   The Federal Emergency Management Agency (FEMA) is responsible for creating and updating flood maps for all the United States. These maps indicate where flooding is most likely to occur and over what period of time. The FEMA maps indicate areas in the 50-, 100-, and 200-year flood zones as well as flood fringe areas. Areas that were not considered in a flood area—flood zone— may now be. Areas that were in a flood zone may no longer be so classified.

Of course no one wants to build a development where it will likely be flooded. There are many restrictions on building in a flood zone or flood fringe area. Floor elevations must be higher, and certain uses may not be allowed. In some areas, no structures at all will be allowed.

In addition to use constraints and increased building costs, lenders may limit the amount or availability of real estate loans in flood areas. Separate flood insurance may be required. Sometimes flood insurance is not available or may be cost-prohibitive. The access to a site may be in a flood zone area, thus impacting the value and use of a site.

Soils.   In addition to having a site out of the flood areas with the appropriate topography, the type of soil is an important consideration. A soil suitability analysis may be necessary if the exact type of soil is unknown. This analysis will report on the following soil characteristics.

Compaction.   An important soil characteristic is **compaction**. How well does the soil compact to make a firm base for the foundation of the buildings? Because some soil does not compact well, it cannot support much weight or requires that elaborate foundations be constructed. For example, the soil may be too sandy and not provide a firm base for a five-story building. In order to construct the building, pilings (concrete posts) may have to be driven into the ground many feet—20, 40, 60 feet, or more! Once these hit a solid surface, perhaps bedrock, they can serve as the support to the foundation of the building. Without the pilings, the foundation could shift with the sand. Think of putting a sheet of thin plywood on a sandy surface. Walk on it enough and what will happen? Eventually the plywood will start moving and then crack. The same thing will happen with the foundation of a building. Once the foundation fails, it is just a matter of time before the building fails by cracking or even collapsing.

Another example is soil which will not dry out. Wet soil (one type is referred to as *bull tallow*) is slippery and will allow the foundation to move, creating the same problem as described above.

If the problem area is small enough, it may be possible to dig out the bad soil and replace it with good soil. Soil replacement takes time and money but may be the best remedy.

Percolation. Here's a question all land brokers ask: "Does it perc?" **Percolation** refers to the soil's ability to absorb water, a characteristic that is critical when installing a septic system because the water needs to drain on the site. If the drain field fails (too much water for the soil to handle), then sewage can contaminate the site because the system failed. This has a severe impact on the wells on the site and surrounding sites.

Even if the property is served by city or county water and sewer systems, it is important that the site be able to handle its own water runoff. As stated earlier, the absorption of water into the ground is one way nature cleanses it. Sites with absorption problems may also suffer erosion and damage from water constantly flowing over the site.

Site configuration. The shape of the site can be more important than the overall size. Narrow areas may be unbuildable. Sites too deep may create circulation or visibility problems. It all gets down to the plan for the site. When we talk about the different types of development, site configuration will be a key component.

Encroachments. An **encroachment** occurs when something "trespasses" on a site (see Figure 4.6). The encroachment can be a fence, a building, or even the building on its own site! Yes, a building can encroach into its setback, side yard, or rear yard. Encroachment here just means that the building is built too close to its boundaries.

Figure 4.6 | Encroachment

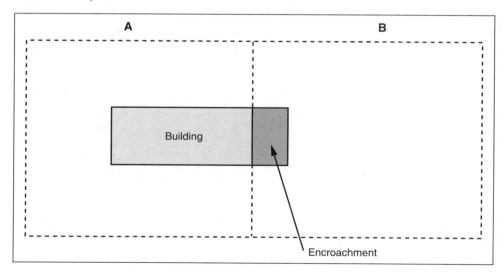

To solve an encroachment problem, a developer may

- remove the encroaching item (e.g., knock down the fence);
- purchase the land being encroached upon;
- request a variance from the zoning department (in the case of encroaching outside of the allowable buildable area); or
- negotiate an easement from the owner of the land being encroached upon.

Surveys are done to determine property boundaries and to ascertain whether any encroachments are in evidence.

■ Summary

So it all begins with the land. Sometimes it stops there, and sometimes it doesn't. Many times, once a development is built, most, if not all, of the land issues have been addressed. For example, the zoning is correct for the type of use being developed. However, if a buyer wishes to change the use, the zoning may have to be changed too. A new use may have an impact on the environment of the site or surrounding areas. By knowing what to consider, a savvy commercial broker can advise a buyer or seller on what to expect.

For more information on land brokerage, visit the REALTORS® Land Institute website at www.rliland.com.

case study   Highest and Best Use

Use your knowledge of highest and best use to solve the following problem. Several developers have come to you looking for land. Each has a different product, as follows:

- One is an apartment developer, building a 300-unit upscale development.
- One is a shopping center developer, building a 100,000-square-foot shopping center with a grocery store and other upscale, specialty shops. A drugstore will be freestanding on the corner.
- One is an office building developer, building a 150,000-square-foot call center for a large bank. It will be a self-contained facility with a cafeteria and operating 24/7. Security is high.

You have a site and have listed its six major attributes. For each developer, indicate the two most important attributes (an attribute can be of importance to more than one developer).

Attributes	Apartment	Shopping Center	Office
Great visibility			
On a bus line			
In a desirable school district			
On the "going toward home" side of the road			
Fairly flat site			
In a foreign trade zone (FTZ)			

■ Review Questions

1. A cellular phone company wants to place a cell tower in a busy city. Which rights are *MOST* applicable to them?
   a. Subsurface rights
   b. Mineral rights
   c. Air rights
   d. Water rights

2. A farmer with acres of crops would be *MOST* interested in which of the following rights?
   a. Subsurface rights
   b. Mineral rights
   c. Air rights
   d. Water rights

3. Last year, a neighbor built his fence on your property by accident. This is an example of
   a. an encroachment.
   b. an easement.
   c. a lien.
   d. adverse possession.

4. The local power company has been asked to supply electricity to your newly built home. What gives them the right to put lines and poles on your property?
   a. Encroachment
   b. Easement
   c. Lien
   d. Adverse possession

5. You are looking at a piece of land. What tests will you likely perform?
   a. Compaction
   b. Percolation
   c. Environmental
   d. All of these

chapter five

Commercial Contracts

overview

No book on commercial real estate would be complete without a discussion of the contracts used. A true meeting of the minds, necessary for a contract to be enforceable, needs a written agreement. When acting as an agent, a broker must understand all parts of the agreement so the broker can best advise a client. Some contracts are short and simple; others are long and complex. We will look at the key elements in sales contracts and leases. ■

learning objectives

When you have completed this chapter, you will be able to

- describe different lease terms, and
- report the effect lease terms have on value.

■ Key Terms

common area maintenance (CAM)	confidentiality agreement	letter of intent (LOI)
	due diligence	option
conditional contract	estoppel certificate	standstill agreement

■ A Note on Sample Contracts

There will not be sample contracts in this book because states have different legal requirements that may need to be included in (or omitted from) a real estate contract. Leaving out (or including) such a requirement may create an unenforceable contract or even expose the buyer or seller to liability. It is critical that an experienced real estate attorney is used when creating or reviewing a commercial lease.

About Contracts

We don't know what we don't know. It seems easy to summarize those business terms we understand and have agreed to, but what about those things not contemplated, such as what happens if the property is taken through eminent domain or suffers a total or (more complex) a partial loss? What if the seller or buyer dies before closing? What if there is a problem discovered during the inspection that was not contemplated in the contract?

When we act as our own broker or attorney, we have limited perspective because we are seeing it from only our point of view. It's best to have an attorney assist with contract preparation and review to have an unbiased opinion. In addition, your real estate attorney can identify potential problems and address them in your contract. Just make sure that the attorney you use specializes in the type of transaction that you are doing.

Some REALTOR® associations have standard form contracts with "fill in the blanks" for their members. Check with your local association.

Caution!

Even though there may be a standard form contract in your area, it is important to understand all of the clauses and the impact they will have on your client. Consult an experienced real estate attorney for advice.

It is easy to overlook what isn't there. When negotiating contracts and leases, we can develop tunnel vision and overlook seemingly unimportant clauses. I've learned that those overlooked unimportant clauses can become important quickly. Following is an example from my own experience:

> We leased a floor of our office building in South Carolina to a large national company. The tenant insisted that we use their lease agreement rather than ours. With a large regional or national tenant, this is common. While we'd rather use our lease agreement (it was pro-landlord—us), the tenant made using theirs a condition of the agreement, what we refer to as a "deal breaker."
>
> We used their lease, and our attorney and I carefully reviewed it. We did counter some of the clauses and eventually reached agreement on the lease they sent to us.
>
> All went well until it was time for us to refinance the building—about three years into the lease. The lender required that we have all tenants (especially the large ones) sign a form, called an **estoppel certificate** (used to have the tenant ratify the terms of their lease; it provides proof to others such as buyers or lenders that the lease they are reviewing is the actual lease the tenant executed). This is a standard clause in every lease because any buyer or lender would want ratification of the existing lease. I requested that the tenant execute the estoppel certificate, and, to my surprise, they declined. I reminded them that it was a requirement of their lease and they suggested that I reread the lease. When I did, I discovered to my utter horror that there was no such requirement in their lease. Because the request for an estoppel certificate is a landlord issue, a tenant wouldn't need it and would not include it in their lease unless asked by the landlord.
>
> All turned out all right, though it cost me some new carpet and paint— yes, I ended up bribing the tenant to sign the estoppel. It taught all of us

a valuable lesson—it's easy to analyze what is there but more difficult to notice what's not there. Lesson learned: Read the lease, then read it again. Take a break and read it again, and so on.

For the three contracts discussed in this chapter—the contract for sale of property, the lease agreement, and the property management agreement—I will list essential elements and give a brief description. I now use a checklist when reviewing someone else's lease. I cross off clause titles from my list as I review them and then look to see what's left. Because some of the clause titles on my list aren't relevant to a particular contract, they can be crossed off. What's left needs to be added to the contract. Had I had such a list when negotiating the lease in the previous example, "estoppel" would have stood out like a sore thumb, and we could have easily added it. I feel sure that the tenant wouldn't have contested it because the clause is important for the owner and widely accepted in the industry.

■ Contract for Sale of Property

Letters of Intent

Before you begin negotiations on your contract, you may elect to use a letter of intent. The **letter of intent (LOI)** is a way for the parties to negotiate business terms without anything being binding. It's typically done in letter format on either party's letterhead with the key terms desired. Take care to avoid having anything in the letter of intent that may be enforceable, as in some states the letter of intent could be considered to be a contract. It does not matter what you call it: If it looks like a contract, then a court may rule it as such. Things that may cause your letter of intent to transform into a contract are discussed below.

Standstill agreement. The **standstill agreement** requires the seller to not market the property or negotiate with any other parties while the seller is negotiating with the buyer. It could work the other way too, where a buyer cannot negotiate on any competing properties while they are negotiating with the seller.

Confidentiality agreement. The **confidentiality agreement** requires that neither party discuss any aspect of the transaction or distribute any materials relating to the transaction. Sometimes the seller will require that any materials sent to a prospective buyer be returned.

Injunctive relief/damages. The injunctive relief/damages agreement spells out any penalties for violating the above.

As you can see, the letter of intent can easily fall into a contract when there are enforceable provisions. In any case, you don't want to create an ambiguous document.

Remember, if you have to go to court, you've lost even if you win. The only ones who make a living by being in court are those in the legal profession!

On a complex transaction, a letter of intent saves redrafting of the contract by attorneys. Once the terms are reached, the letter of intent can then be used as the framework of the contract. Remember that nothing is binding until the actual contract is properly executed. Even if the other party agreed to everything in your letter of intent, nothing forces that party to execute the contract if they change their mind. However, those in the business rely on the "good faith" of those they are dealing with. If a buyer, seller, landlord, or tenant continues to disaffirm their letter of intent, it can impair their ability to negotiate in the future. Word travels fast.

Key Clauses in Contract for Sale of Property

Discussed below are the key clauses in a contract for the sale of property.

Parties.   All of the buyers and all of the sellers must be listed. It sounds simple, but it's not!

Let's start with the buyers. What type of entity is buying the property? Individual, partnership, limited liability company (LLC), sub-S corporation, or C corporation? In the case of an entity other than individuals, who has the authority to sign the contract? There have been many incidents of contracts executed by an employee of a company who did not have authority to sign the contract. The courts may or may not rule that contract enforceable. Do you want to take this risk? At the very least, you will have to spend time and money to resolve it. Most people involved in real estate transactions don't have extra time available or extra money to spend. There are documents that show who has the authority to contract on behalf of the entity. Your real estate attorney can assist you with this. Another issue is the correct listing of the entity. There is a difference between "ABC Stores" and "ABC Stores, Inc." Also, many people purchase property in a named partnership or LLC, such as Chandler, Dearborn III, LLC. That will be very different from Chandler, Dearborn II, LLC. Check the documentation.

Now, on to the sellers. This section of the contract can be even more dangerous than the buyer section if done incorrectly. If all the sellers are not listed on the contract and if all the sellers do not sign the contract, you may not have a contract at all. A seller can only sell what they have, as seen in the following example.

A real estate colleague of mine, Char, listed a property owned (she thought) by a sweet elderly lady. Char worked very hard to market the property, using her own funds. When she finally found a buyer, she gleefully brought the offer to her client, who said, "Well, my dear, I need to run this by my brother in California." It's not uncommon for people to ask others for advice. Char impressed upon the seller the need for haste. A few days later, the client said that her brother wasn't impressed by the offer; although, she liked it a lot and needed the money. Char encouraged her to proceed, assuring her it was a good offer. Her elderly client explained that it wasn't her decision to make because her brother owned 66% of the property! When Char took the listing, she pulled the deed and saw only one name on it. It turned out that the client borrowed money from her brother and gave him a two-thirds interest in the property as collateral. Because she had never repaid the loan, he still had that interest. Char just pulled the deed—she didn't do complete title work. Should she have done more? It depends. There are different practices throughout the country. Now, had there been red flags—that is, items that just don't seem right—Char might have pursued it or had an attorney do so.

Here is another example from my own experience. I was buying property from a man who said he was single. Later on I heard he wasn't. In North Carolina, a spouse has a "marital life estate interest" in real property owned by the other spouse. It can get complicated, but what it means is that it takes only one to buy but two to sell. When I discovered this, I required that he get his wife's signature on the contract. It was a real problem as they were "sort of" separated. However, it would have been a bigger problem at closing because he would not have been able to deliver clear title. As with the buyer names, be sure you have all the correct seller names or entity name(s). James L. Smith II is a different person than James L. Smith III.

Property description.   Exactly what is being conveyed? A legal description of the property is a must. An address alone does not describe the size of the lot, improvements on the lot, and so on. There are different ways to describe a property, such as a metes-and-bounds description done by a surveyor or, in most states, the government rectangular survey system. Ask your attorney the best way to describe property in your area. Using a tax identification number or a tax map is acceptable only if you feel the tax records are 100% accurate. Referring to any document other than a legal description done for the sale is only as good as that description. For example, say you were buying 25 acres. You look at the deed the seller received when she bought the property and use the legal description from the deed. That's fine as long as you are entirely sure that the deed description is accurate and the seller hasn't sold or given any of it away. Why save a few dollars on something so important as knowing what you're buying?

You also need to know what city, county, or jurisdiction the property is in. There might be special restrictions, zoning regulations, taxing authorities, and so on that can affect your decision.

Along with the property description, make sure to include any easements or rights-of-way. I just heard from a real estate broker that a potential client of his discovered that they sold the only access to their 200 acres, and now the 200 acres is nearly worthless because of that access problem. Of course, when they sold the house (which had the access to the remaining 200 acres) they didn't use a REAL-TOR® or a real estate attorney. They wanted to save a few dollars. This is another reason to have experienced, unbiased eyes review any agreements.

Along with the description, there may be an attachment showing the property. Make sure the attachment is referenced in the contract and make sure the attachment and the description agree. I once sold a lot and described it by subdivision plat number and date, deed book number, lot and block number—standard practice in my area for this type of sale. I attached a plat of the subdivision and accidentally marked the wrong lot. Now we have an "ambiguity," which is not good. Which lot is it? We worked it out, but it could have been a problem costing time and money.

Purchase price.   The purchase price is the agreed-upon price in dollars. Now, how is it to be paid?

Earnest money.   A good faith deposit the buyer makes at the time of the offer is referred to as earnest money. Once a contract (agreement) is reached, the earnest money is typically held throughout the transaction by one of the agents, the seller, an escrow company, or an attorney. Decide how much earnest money is to be paid and by when. Typically it will be applied to the purchase price at closing. Decide who will hold the earnest money. Most, if not all, states have laws governing the handling of earnest money when held by real estate brokers. How much should the earnest money be? There is no national rule of thumb. If you are the buyer, then you want to pay little. If you are the seller, then you want a lot. If the buyer defaults, the earnest money typically goes to the seller. The contract needs to state what happens to the earnest money.

Proceeds of a loan.   If the contract is contingent upon the buyer being able to secure funds from a lender, then the contract needs to state the loan terms and time allowed. If you are the buyer, then you want as much flexibility as possible (you might insert wording such as, "Contingent upon buyer finding funds at terms suitable to buyer…"). If you are the seller, then you want to hold the buyer's feet to the fire (you'd want to spell out the terms specifically, such as, "$____ amount, with a term of not less than ___ years at an interest rate not above ___%, with points not to exceed ___"). While it may be typical that the buyer pay all loan costs in a commercial transaction, your contract should so state that.

Loan to be assumed.   If the contract is contingent upon the seller's loan being assumed, all terms relevant to the assumption must be listed. For example, I bought a shopping center in Virginia, subject to assuming the seller's existing loan. It has an attractive interest rate and because of some redevelopment issues, an assumption would be faster, less expensive, and easier. Imagine my surprise when the lender advised me that the loan could be assumed for one point (1% of the loan's outstanding balance), but the interest rate would go to "market rate," which was 3% higher than it was currently! That wasn't our deal. The seller assured me that I could assume at par (same rate). Fortunately, the seller stepped in and cleared things up with the bank. Had the seller not had that relationship with the local bank, the higher rates would have been a deal breaker.

Seller financing.   If the contract is contingent upon the seller financing part or all of the purchase price, all terms and documentation required must be covered in the contract. Be sure to have an attorney involved in all aspects of seller financing. State laws can impact how this is done.

Cash.   List the amount of cash the buyer plans to bring to closing. The earnest money, loan proceeds, assumed loan amount, seller financing, and cash must add up to the purchase price. Terms are every bit as important as price. For example: You want a quick sale because you need the cash for another investment in 90 days. You receive three offers. One is all cash for $1 million. Another is contingent upon the buyer getting 90% financing (unusual in commercial deals) at attractive interest rates. The purchase price is $1.1 million. The third offer is contingent upon seller financing and is for $1.25 million. Which offer is best? It depends on how badly you need that cash and if you have another resource for funds. Also it depends on how likely you think it is that the buyer will get the 90% loan and how confident you are that the third buyer will pay on time. Sometimes cash in hand is the way to go.

Closing date.   Define what *closing* means. Is it signing the deed? Is it transferring funds? Is it recording the deed? Or is it when the deed is delivered to the escrow agent? There are local practices. Your escrow agent or attorney will advise you on how it's typically done. Of course, you can define it any way you want, but state laws or regulations may limit your options. Also, indicate where closing occurs. In a "closing meeting" state, parties meet at someone's office (usually an attorney's), sign documents, and then transfer money. In an "escrow" state, parties drop off signed documents at the escrow agent's office and are notified when the closing is complete.

Inspections and inspection period.   This is the period of time where the buyer is to complete any inspections of the property. These include physical and nonphysical inspections, such as checking on the zoning, completing feasibility studies, and other **due diligence** items (see the appendix). The buyer needs to allow enough time to complete inspections and make a decision on the property.

Real estate agents involved.   Unless state law dictates otherwise, list any real estate agents involved, who they represent, if anyone, and their companies.

Notice addresses.   List the official address of the sellers and buyers. Where should notices be sent and to whom should they be addressed?

Intended use of the property.   The intended use statement may be placed in the inspections clause, particularly if the use is to change, but in my opinion, the intended use clause is one of the most important clauses in the contract. State the intended use of the property here (office building, shopping center, apartments). Either here or in the seller affidavit clause, require the seller to certify that the seller does not know of any regulation that prohibits the intended use. Depending on whether you are the buyer or seller, the wording will change. A buyer may want the wording of intended use to be specific or may not want to reveal anything at all. A seller will want it broad, if it's a contingency of the contract. Let's look at a couple of examples.

Developer Vic wants to buy a tract of land for a Walmart Supercenter. If he can't develop a Walmart Supercenter there, he's not interested in the land. That's all he develops. While he is negotiating with the seller, he may not want the seller to know it's a Walmart, or Walmart may not want it known. In that case, he may write in "retail" or "shopping center" in the use clause. The land is zoned for retail, but the town requires a special use permit for any retail building over 100,000 square feet or for any 24-hour facility. Before closing, Vic attends the hearing for his special use permit and it is denied. Can Vic walk away based on the use clause? He probably cannot because the property can be used for retail, just not the retail Vic wants. Now, if Vic had made the contract conditioned upon being able to develop the Walmart Supercenter, then he might have an out when the special use permit was denied.

Apartment developer Ronnie wants to buy a tract of land for the development of 250 apartments. The land is zoned multifamily and will support the density Ronnie wants. However, a former owner placed a deed restriction on the land that prohibits development near the lake on the property. That would eliminate 50 units. If Ronnie has just specified "apartments" or "multifamily" use as a condition, he would not be released from the contract based on the use clause because he could still develop it with apartments—but not as many.

Developer Ronnie was saved by his inspection clause. He found out about the deed restriction, tried to work it out, but was unable to do so during his inspection period. Developer Vic wasn't so lucky. He was obligated to purchase the property as the special use permit request was denied after his inspection period had expired. Unless his contract gave him some other out, he may well be required to proceed with the closing.

Payment and proration of costs.   List how expenses will be prorated and who pays for what. For example, how will real estate taxes be prorated? Who pays for deed preparation? If the property being sold is an income-producing property, how will rents be handled? Who will pay expenses such as utilities?

Documents.   List any and all documents the buyers need in order to make their decisions and complete their inspections. On an income-producing property, these documents would include copies of leases, contracts, surveys, deeds, restrictive covenants, title policies, and so on. On land, it might include any soil reports, environmental reports, topographical maps, et cetera. List when these documents are due to the buyer, and if there is a cost to copy or produce, who pays that cost. In the event the buyer doesn't buy, are the documents to be returned to the seller?

Quality of title.   List the type and quality of title the seller is to convey (usually fee simple marketable and insurable) and the type of deed to be used. Some use a general warranty deed and others may prefer a special warranty deed. There are many other types of deeds depending on the state and transaction. Have your real estate attorney explain the differences and advise you about the best to use.

Conditions/contingencies.   There are two types of contracts commonly used in the purchase of commercial real estate: **conditional contracts** and **options**. A conditional contract says that the buyer agrees to buy at the terms stated "so long as" the following conditions are met. Then conditions are listed, such as proper zoning, soil conditions suitable for building, et cetera. By contrast, under an option, the buyer has a set amount of time to perform any inspections. At the end of the period, the buyer must decide to move ahead or not. If the buyer moves ahead, it is under the agreed-upon terms of the contract. If the buyer elects to cancel, then the earnest money is handled in accordance with the contract. These two ways of thinking are vastly different. In a conditional contract, the buyer has agreed to buy, as long as everything checks out. In an option contract, the buyer makes no promises, but the seller is obligated to sell under the terms of the agreement. One contract is not necessarily better than the other; different markets just use different types. While the option contract gives the buyer more flexibility, a buyer may spend thousands of dollars performing due diligence and will only cancel if there is a problem going forward. In addition, the buyer has spent valuable time working on the property inspections—time the buyer could have spent on a profitable property instead.

The conditions/contingencies section is the "meat" of a conditional contract. This is where all the contingencies are listed. Without going into a lot of detail, we describe below some of the typical conditions. Of course any condition can be added to suit the transaction.

Loan.   If the buyer can't get the loan they need, then the buyer is not obligated to purchase the property.

Title.   If the seller cannot deliver the quality of title specified, then the buyer can cancel.

Use.   Use was discussed earlier in the "Intended Use of the Property" section. If the buyer cannot use the property as defined, then the buyer can cancel.

Condition of property.   If the property isn't in the same condition at closing as it was at some earlier point in time (usually at the time of the contract or offer), then the buyer can cancel.

Inspections/due diligence.   If the buyer is not satisfied with the outcome of any inspections made, then the buyer can cancel. If the desired outcome is specified (e.g., the soil was to be suitable for a three-story office building and parking lot), then it is most likely a conditional contract. If it's not specified, then it's probably a form of an option contract. Further, the buyer needs to have the right to enter the property to make inspections, perform soil tests, et cetera. If the inspections include inspecting the leases and books of the property, then the requirements and timing need to be listed in the contract. Rezoning also falls in this area.

Environmental.   In today's market, the environmental section is often extensive. In addition to being able to perform environmental inspections, the seller may be asked to represent or warrant that it has no actual knowledge of any environmental problems. The best source for in-depth information is a local environmental engineer.

Earnest money disbursement.   Often influenced by state law when the money is held by a real estate broker, the contract must state how earnest money will be handled and what constitutes a forfeiture.

Loss/damage.   Describe what happens when a loss or damage occurs. For example, between contract and closing, a fire guts a small part of the building. What happens now? Is the buyer still obligated to buy? Must the seller repair the fire damage?

Notices.   How are notices handled? In person and certified mail are most common.

Seller knowledge.   I'm grouping several things here under seller knowledge. In some place in the contract, a buyer will want to have the seller affirm that the seller has no negative information that impacts the usability or value of the property. For example, the seller may know that the grocery store is going to close, and its closing would devalue the shopping center. The "seller knowledge" clause would require that the sellers not withhold information such as this. Other issues asked of the seller might include the following:

- Restrictive covenants
- Deed restrictions
- Condemnation
- Lawsuits against the property or key tenants
- Assessments
- Compliance with laws and ordinances
- Liens

Memorandum of contract.   Can this contract be recorded and, if so, what form is to be used?

Proper signature blocks.   Your attorney will provide these.

There are many other important clauses in a contract, but those will be covered by your experienced real estate attorney. I covered mainly the business-related clauses here—the issues a buyer or seller needs to consider before agreeing to any contract.

Before we move on to commercial leases, let's take a quick look back at the steps the parties typically take before the contract is signed.

The Sales Process

We know the terms and how they will be negotiated; now let's look at the process from sale to closing.

Step 1.   Assure that the buyer and seller are who they say they are and have the capacity to contract.

Step 2.   Buyer and seller negotiate and conclude with a signed contract to purchase.

Step 3. The seller may have certain items to deliver to buyer during the inspection period (referred to as the due diligence period). These items could include the following:

- Title information
- Service contracts
- Leases
- Estoppel certificates
- Survey
- Environmental studies and reports
- Inspection reports

Step 4. The buyer performs due diligence. This covers inspections they want to complete and all investigations they need to make. The buyer needs to have enough time to investigate everything plus enough time to negotiate the solution of problems found with the seller. In some cases this might include procuring a financing commitment.

The appendix contains a list of possible due diligence items. Depending on the property, the use, and the buyer, some items may not be performed.

The earlier examples with developers Vic and Ronnie illustrate the importance of performing necessary due diligence within the time allowed.

Step 5. The buyer will undoubtedly find some problems that will need to be negotiated with the seller. For example, termite damage may be discovered that significantly impacts the usability and stability of the building. It depends on how the contract is written. Usually, if there is a due diligence clause, the buyer either has the right to not proceed (for any reason) or the buyer has the right to not proceed if he discovers any adverse facts during the inspections. Given this, the buyer would tell the seller that they do not want to proceed with the sale, unless the seller then decides whether to make repairs, allow more time for due diligence, lower the price, or allow the buyer to walk away, with the seller then putting the property back on the market. Let's say, for example, that the seller agrees to reduce the price.

Step 6. The contract is amended.

Step 7. The buyer secures a loan commitment letter (discussed in Chapter 7) prior to closing.

Step 8. The attorneys draw up all closing documents. The lender is notified.

Step 9. Closing occurs; money and title are transferred; and the brokers are paid. This is done in a closing meeting or through an escrow or title company.

■ Commercial Leases

The value of a property is frequently determined by the quality of the tenant and the terms of the lease. From the tenant's point of view, the lease allows them to have control over the space and dictates their costs. Every part of a lease must be reviewed to ensure that a true meeting of the minds has taken place. Be sure to involve an experienced real estate attorney.

Commercial leases vary a great deal, depending on the situation. For example, a landlord may have a 1,500-square-foot space ready for move in. The lease may be 5 pages or 50 pages depending on the agreement of the parties. In this example, the average lease would be 5 to 10 pages.

As we did with the commercial contract for sale of property, we'll list important lease clauses to consider. I'll focus on the business issues and won't be able to go into the detail necessary for an informed decision about an actual transaction. For that, please acquire the services of an experienced commercial broker and your real estate attorney.

Note that these terms are listed in the order one might find them in a lease.

Commercial Lease Terms

Date of lease.   Specify the date the lease is executed. Specificity is important because other clauses may tie to this date.

Names of landlord and tenant.   It is important to get the names right. It is also critical to know if the person signing the lease is empowered to do so. For example, a well-known developer executed a lease with an international firm and started construction on the space. Partway through the process, the tenant's supervisor came to visit. During the tour of the soon-to-be new space, the supervisor remarked that the employee who executed the lease on behalf of the company did not have any authority to do so. He further said that the company's legal staff felt that the lease was unenforceable because of this fact and that the company wasn't sure it wanted this space (this is what we call "playing hardball"). The developer was obviously rattled and concerned about the future of this unfinished custom and expensive space. Fortunately, the company and the developer worked things out. However, the result could have spelled disaster for both parties. Lesson learned: Know with whom you are dealing.

Premises.   What is being leased must be adequately described. You need an address at a minimum and a legal description. An exhibit may be attached. Make sure that any written description agrees with the attachment. For example, several years ago, a company called on tenants of a shopping center. The company implied that it could save the tenant money by auditing its lease and finding landlord errors. The fee to the company would be half of any monies saved by the tenant. Well, when the company measured the space, they found that square footage was overreported in the lease. Because rent and pass-through expenses were based on the square footage, this affected the tenant's costs. The tenant sent a demand letter to the landlord requesting a refund for the overpayment over the past five years. The amount was in the thousands of dollars! The company then checked other tenants in the center and found their space to be misreported—some over and some under. Of course, those under did not voluntarily come forward, but those who were over did come forward, and this caused havoc for the landlord.

Term.   State the length of the lease. This should include beginning and ending dates. It is important to define the term so that any rent increases, adjustments, and so on can be done on a timely basis. In lieu of actual dates, the term may be defined by number of months or years. In this case, it is important to agree on the lease commencement date, as the ending date will be tied to it.

Rent.   Define the rental amount and when it is due. You may also add any rent increases or adjustment in this section. If any index is used, define which one it is (e.g., Consumer Price Index, Urban Wage Earners and Clerical Worker, All Cities,

CPI-W, 1982–1984 = 100). Define how and when any increase in the consumer price index (CPI) is calculated. You may also show any late charges in this section. In some retail leases, a percentage of gross sales may be due as additional rent, referred to as *percentage rent*. This charge needs to be carefully explained so that all parties know how it is calculated and when it is due. If rent is calculated on square footage, explain how it is calculated.

Additional rent may include percentage rent, pass-through expenses, such as common area expenses, real estate taxes, insurance, and utilities.

Rent commencement. Rent commencement may be triggered by any number of events. It may be when the tenant occupies the property, when the lease begins, when the tenant opens for business, or a set date. The lease needs to be specific about when rent is due and when it starts.

Notices. Include where rent is to be sent and where any notices are to be sent to landlord or tenant.

Security deposit. Because most states regulate security deposits handled by real estate brokers in some fashion, follow state regulations. At the very least, show how much the deposit is, who is holding it, and how and when it will be returned to the tenant.

Costs paid by landlord and tenant. It is very important to detail who pays what. For example, it's important to address who pays each of the following:

- Utilities
- Taxes
- Insurance
- Maintenance
- Landscaping
- Signage
- Trash collection
- Janitorial

Common areas. In a building where there are multiple tenants, define what the common area is (sidewalks, driveways, parking lots, open spaces) and define how the tenant may use the common areas. For example, can a tenant put goods for sale on the sidewalk? In larger developments, there may be "rules and regulations" attachments that spell out all of this. This information is important because common area maintenance expenses will be affected by the area covered.

Common area maintenance expenses. If a tenant is paying the operating costs of a shopping center on a pro rata basis, then it is important to define the tenant's share in percentage terms and how the **common area maintenance (CAM)** expenses are calculated (see Chapter 9).

Use of premises. This is one of the most important clauses for both the landlord and the tenant. As a landlord, carefully define the allowed uses by the tenant. For example, if this is a shopping center and you've leased to a nail salon, you probably don't want them to open a restaurant in part of their space. In some cases, you may have given a tenant an "exclusive," meaning that you won't allow any other tenants to have that same use. The following is an example illustrating the importance of the clause that spells out the use of the premises.

Several years ago, in a shopping center I was developing, we gave a video store an exclusive to offer videos for rent or sale. The grocery and drugstores were excluded from this restriction. The video store owner wasn't worried about the few videos the grocery and drugstore sold. Well, the tanning salon started offering videos on tanning. Again, the video store owner wasn't worried. Then the tanning salon offered exercise videos. Then they added other videos. Suddenly, it was hard to tell if they were a tanning salon or a video store. The video store owner complained, and we had to enforce the use clause of the tanning salon and had to prohibit the salon from selling or renting videos.

Most landlords and owners place a high value on the use clause because it can impact the retail mix of services of a shopping center, influence parking, create noxious odors, bring in heavy traffic to the building, or cause unwanted publicity to the building.

From the tenants' perspective, they want as much flexibility as possible to sell or do the type of business they want. If they want an exclusive, then it is very important to adequately define it. Again, here is an example of the importance of the "use of premises" clause.

At a shopping center in North Carolina, we had both a regional supermarket and a specialty foods market. The specialty market had many restrictions prohibiting them from selling "typical" grocery items that would compete with the supermarket. While they could sell a very small percentage of items found in the supermarket, this wasn't a problem for the supermarket because the specialty market was known for organic items not found in a typical supermarket. As time went on, the specialty market kept adding more and more "typical" grocery items due to requests from customers. It was easier to get in and out of the market, and while they certainly charged more than the supermarket did, they found that the items kept selling.

On July 3, I got a call at home from the supermarket manager. "The specialty market is selling watermelons on the sidewalk,"—both stores were prohibited from sidewalk selling—and, "Make them stop! Also, they have too many grocery items in their store." I called the specialty market and asked if they were selling the forbidden watermelons on the sidewalk. It turns out the melons were organic, seedless melons that cost three times those from the supermarket. The market promised to bring the melons inside by 6:00 pm that day. So, I called the supermarket manager back to report what I'd been told and to give him permission to put his watermelons on the sidewalk that day. The supermarket manager called me back in about an hour to report that he bought one of the seedless melons from the specialty market and they were not seedless—he found several seeds. Yes, they were much more expensive, but it was another case of that specialty market lying about their goods.

Eventually, this all evolved into a watermelon fight on the sidewalk. The stationery store called to report it. By the time I got in touch with the fruit-throwing parties, the event was over and the sidewalk was cleaned. So can the use clause be important? Yes!

Insurance.   The tenant will need to have insurance on their store or office contents as well as liability coverage. The lease needs to specify the minimum amounts and allow the landlord to receive a copy and be named as additional insured.

Repairs.   The lease must specify who will fix what and what standards will be used. For example, if the tenants are responsible for the air-conditioning equipment, must they use a licensed contractor to handle any repairs or can one of the tenants' handy brother-in-law do the repairs? If the landlord is to make repairs, how is notice handled and how soon after notice must the landlord respond? What about the right of "self-help," where the tenants fix a problem then deduct the cost from the rent? Is that permitted?

Alterations.   Is the tenant allowed to make changes to the space? Can they add outlets? Do they need permission? Again, it depends on whether you are the landlord or the tenant. The tenants may want the right to do whatever they want in their space, but the landlord will be concerned about the quality of the contractors, violations of any warranties, damage to the building systems, and so on. Also, must the tenant restore the premises to their original move-in condition when they move out? How about trade fixtures, such as equipment and lighting? Must the tenant restore the building to its original condition?

Condemnation.   What happens if the building or tenant space is partially or fully condemned? What are the tenants' rights?

Assignment or subletting.   Can tenants assign their lease to another business? Do they need the landlord's approval? How about leasing part of their space to another business? What happens if the tenant profits on the subletting? Should the landlord get part or all of that profit? As you've probably guessed by now, the way this clause is worded depends on who is in the stronger position—the landlord or the tenant.

Default.   What constitutes default? Usually it is nonpayment of monies owed or a violation of any of the provisions of the lease, such as use, insurance, rules and regulations, repairs, and so on.

Remedies upon default.   What is the process once a tenant is in default? Again, state law or local practice may dictate how this is handled. There will always be a required notice period, and the tenant will be given time to "cure" the default. If they don't, then the lease will state the process for remedies available to the landlord, which typically includes terminating the lease and evicting the tenant.

Signage.   The lease must state where tenant signs can be placed and the maximum number and size and that they must comply with any ordinances.

Landlord's right of entry.   The landlord needs to have the right to enter the tenant's space during the lease for routine inspections and maintenance. Without this right in the lease, the landlord may not be legally allowed to enter the tenant's space without the tenant's permission.

Lender's rights.   In the case where the property is financed, the lender may have made certain conditions above the tenant's rights—such as the right to inspect the property and being a first lien on the property. The lender may require that any tenant sign an agreement allowing the lender first position. This is called a *subordination agreement*. It is very important for a lender to be in first place in the event of a loan default, and without this clause, the tenant is under no obligation to subordinate to a lender—either in the present or the future.

Holding over.   The lease must state what happens when a tenants' lease expires and they don't renew but wish to stay on.

Environmental issues.   The lease must instruct the tenant to do nothing that would cause an environmental problem for the property and to acquire any permits needed for their business if they are handling any hazardous materials.

Transfer of landlord's interest.   This clause gives the landlord the right to transfer their interest in the property and binds the tenant to the successor. This clause requires the tenant to execute necessary documents to ratify their lease, such as the estoppel certificate discussed above in an earlier example.

Memorandum of lease.   The parties agree to the form to be used for the tenant's recording of the lease. Seldom would either party want the entire lease recorded into the public records.

Owner's mortgage financing.   Many lenders have requirements made when they make a loan. Leases executed include these requirements.

Tenant trade name.   List the name under which the tenant plans to conduct business.

Marketing/merchant's association.   Is there a marketing fund or a merchant's association? Must the tenant join and contribute? This clause is usually found in shopping center leases.

Acceptance of demised premises.   What constitutes acceptance by the tenant, and what happens when the tenant accepts the space? Does the lease term commence? Does rent start?

Tenant's opening for business.   Does the tenant's opening for business trigger any event such as lease commencement or rent due?

Tenant guarantee.   Must any principals of the tenant's business personally guarantee the lease? Is the tenant part of a parent corporation?

Definition of gross sales.   Gross sales are used for calculation of percentage rent. What counts and what is deducted from gross sales? The clause may request state sales tax reports to verify sales. Refer to industry guides, such as *Dollars & Cents of Shopping Centers*, published by the International Council of Shopping Centers (ICSC) (see www.icsc.org/publications/item/dollars-cents-of-shopping-centers-the-score-2008-book/).

Statement of gross sales.   As a landlord, even if you think you will never see any percentage rent, you want to see the tenants' sales reports. Why? So you can see how they are doing. If sales are flat or dropping or not at a profitable level, you may want to suggest the tenant confer with a consultant.

Parking.   Stipulate any parking that may be available for tenants and their customers. Perhaps tenants are required to park in the back or away from the front entrance to allow more spaces for customers. Specify if there is any assigned parking.

Tenant upfitting (also called tenant improvements).   If the space is not to be leased as is, then the lease needs to address who will handle upfitting and pay the costs associated. Also, a schedule must be agreed to so as to avoid conflicts about rent commencement.

Tenant's financial statement. This document may be required by a lender or prudent landlord.

Retail restriction limit. Because a landlord does not want a retail tenant to open a competing store nearby, there may be a restriction on doing so within a specified distance of the center.

Estoppel certificate. The landlord may need the tenant to execute a certificate stating that their lease terms are as shown in the lease and as in full effect and have not been modified. An estoppel certificate is used when refinancing or selling the property.

Brokerage. A lease may refer to any brokers representing the parties. Typically the clause states that these are the only brokers involved in the transaction.

Force majeure. Also known as *acts of war*, this clause stipulates what happens if the development is affected by a war or other circumstances beyond the control of the parties.

ADA compliance. Who is responsible for compliance with the Americans with Disabilities Act? Both parties will want the other to be responsible. However, check with your real estate attorney. A California case ruled that, although the lease required the tenant to make sure the space complied with all laws, the landlord was also responsible to see that the space was accessible.

Expansion rights. Does the tenant have any rights to adjacent space? Specify notices required and time periods involved.

Right of first refusal. Does the tenant have the first rights on any space? If so, what is the process and the notice period?

Right to cancel. Do the tenants have any right to cancel their lease? (Warning: This may create a problem with the property's lender or a buyer.) Some examples of reasons to cancel a lease include the vacancy of another tenant, such as a grocery store, damage to the property, change in the access, and so on.

Again, there are many other lease clauses that may pertain to a transaction. In addition, there are standard lease clauses not listed here, such as "definitions," "entire agreement," "execution," that are important but seldom negotiated. Your real estate attorney will add these according to local practice, market conditions, and state regulations.

We will cover one more agreement in detail—the property management agreement—in Chapter 11.

■ Summary

We've reviewed the key terms of a sales contract, a lease agreement, and will later review a property management agreement. In your commercial brokerage career, you may find that you are working with some contracts and clauses more than others, and that's natural. However, when we get into unfamiliar areas, that's when we can make serious mistakes. Approach every contract as if it's the first time you've seen it.

case study   Office/Retail Space

A friend of a friend who needs office/retail space for a new business has approached you. You have agreed to help this friend of a friend. The facts are as follows:

■ Mrs. Linda Greenwood wishes to open a home décor business where she offers decorating and consulting services and sells wall coverings, paint, and window coverings. She may also have some decorator accessories for sale, space permitting. She was an active decorator 10 years ago, but she gave up her business when she started her family. Her youngest child is now in school, and she wishes to go back into business. In the past, she worked for one of the largest architectural firms in the state, handling all of the interior decoration projects. She has not owned her own business before but has a Small Business Administration loan from the local bank to get started. She is well connected. Her husband is a well-known businessman and has agreed to cosign the lease but only if absolutely necessary. They are well off, financially, and she seems to be a bright businessperson.

■ She is not sure how much space she needs but thinks it is around 1,600 square feet. She feels she can make do with 1,400 to 1,800 square feet, depending on the configuration. She'd like the space as "square" as possible. She's budgeted $50,000 per year on space and can go up to $60,000, but the latter would be a stretch.

■ She would like to be in a retail location as opposed to an office park. She plans on making 60% of her income from sales of wall and window coverings and paint.

■ As new shopping centers are built, space is coming available in the older ones. Linda wants to be where the money lives, and that is where the newer centers are being built. They are more expensive, and the space is in higher demand.

After careful research, you find two choices as outlined in Figure 5.1.

Figure 5.1 | Commercial Options

	Cabbage Corners	North Street Market
Size of Center	25,000 sq. ft.	85,000 sq. ft.
Age of Center	new	15 yrs.
Size of Space	1,700 sq. ft.	1,400 sq. ft.
Width × Depth	20′ × 85′	20′ × 70′
Location	Main Road	Main Road
Av. HH* Income	$62,000	$55,000
# HH w/i 5 mi.	65,000	82,000
Rent/sq. ft.	$32 NNN**	$27 NNN
% Rent	0	5% over Break
Rent Increases	2%/yr	CPI
CAM/sq. ft.***	$1 (fixed)	$1.75
Ins./sq. ft.	$0.50	$0.35
RE tax/sq. ft.	$1.10 (just revised)	$0.95 (up for revaluation)
Marketing/sq. ft.	$0.25	0
TI Allowance****	$10/sq. ft.	0, but 1st mo. rent-free
Tenant Mix	Small, Specialty	Grocery, Drug
Req. Hrs. of Operation	10–6	10–9
Req. Days Open	Mon–Sat.	Mon–Sun.
Landlord Strength	Strong	Strong
Length of Lease	3 yrs. w/no option	3–5 yrs. w/1 option
Lease Guaranty	Linda's business	Linda's business + husband

   * HH = Household
  ** NNN = Triple net (Tenant also pays CAM, real estate taxes, and insurance.)
 *** CAM = Common area maintenance
**** Regarding tenant improvements, Linda estimates that she will need to spend about $18,000 on sheetrock, lighting, and so on, to have her space as she needs it at either center. This is the cost to build out the interior of the space.

1. How much is Linda's total rental obligation for each center?

   _____

   _____

2. Which center appears to be best for her based on demographics and location? Why?

   _____

   _____

3. Which center has the best lease terms?

   _____

   _____

4. What is the breakpoint for percentage rent at North Street Market, first year? To calculate the point at which her sales would cause her to owe percentage rent, divide the annual base rent by the percent stated.

    _____

    _____

5. Name the advantages and disadvantages of each center.

    _____

    _____

6. What else might you want to know before making your recommendation to Linda?

    _____

    _____

■ Review Questions

1. The clause in the contract that pertains to the buyer's right to get the property inspected and to perform tests is called
   a. estoppel.
   b. due diligence.
   c. letter of intent.
   d. subordination.

2. The *BEST* way to prenegotiate contract terms before having a contract drafted is to use a
   a. subordination agreement.
   b. letter of intent.
   c. mediator.
   d. confidentially agreement.

3. If a buyer or seller wants to keep the terms of their contract negotiation private, not to be disclosed to anyone else, what can be used?
   a. Subordination agreement
   b. Letter of intent
   c. Confidentially agreement
   d. Standstill agreement

4. When describing a property in a contract, it's *BEST* to use a
   a. legal description.
   b. address.
   c. reference to another deed.
   d. tax record.

5. Which lease clause addresses a tenant's right to let another user take over a part of the space?
   a. Subordination
   b. Common area
   c. Holding over
   d. Subletting and assignment

6

Math and Valuation

overview

Oh no—math! Relax, it's easy math. In order to truly understand income-producing commercial property, a broker must be able to do some good data gathering and basic analysis. In this chapter, we will look at valuation from all approaches but will focus on the income approach. ■

learning objectives

When you have completed this chapter, you will be able to

- calculate the likely selling or lease price of a property,
- describe different analysis methods,
- calculate net operating income (NOI), and
- describe capitalization rates.

■ Key Terms

capitalization rate (cap rate)

cash flow

cash on cash return

comparable

cost approach

gross rent multiplier (GRM)

income approach

internal rate of return (IRR)

market approach

net operating income (NOI)

net present value (NPV)

operating expenses

■ What's It Worth?

There are three ways to value property: the market or sales comparison approach, the cost approach, and the income approach. We will concentrate on the income approach here. While the primary method we will use here is the capitalization method, we will also look at other measures of investment, such as the internal rate of return, net present value, and the gross rent multiplier.

Be mindful of your state's laws regarding broker price opinions (BPOs) and broker's opinions of value (BOVs). Some states prohibit the use of the term "value" when doing a BPO unless one is a state licensed appraiser. Some states have restrictions on what a real estate licensee can and cannot do when it comes to estimating a price or lease rate.

The Market Approach

The **market approach**, also called *sales comparison approach*, involves estimating value by analyzing other like properties recently sold in the market.

The market approach is used when the broker can find several comparable properties recently sold. Sometimes there are not any recently sold **comparables**. In that case, the broker will need to rely on another method (explained later in this chapter) or use older comparables. The following are the steps involved in the comparison approach to value:

Step 1.   Find several comparable properties (comps) that "recently sold."

Step 2.   Make adjustments to the comps by comparing them to the subject property (the subject property is the one you are trying to value). If the subject property is superior, add the dollar value of the feature to the comp. If the subject property is inferior, subtract the value of the feature from the comp. This may include adjustments based on the quality of the tenant or the lease terms.

Step 3.   Calculate the value per square foot of each comp by analyzing the comps as described above.

Step 4.   Multiply that value by the subject property's square footage.

Step 5.   Make any adjustments for land and location.

For example, Sheila has a listing on a convenience store. In order to price it, she finds four other convenience stores that have sold in the past six months. Three are in similar locations. By comparing her property to the three comparables, Sheila can estimate the value of her seller's property.

The Cost Approach

The **cost approach** involves estimating value by estimating the land value and the cost of replacing improvements.

This approach is relied on when other approaches won't work because the property doesn't have any comparables or an income stream. An appraiser can show you how it is done and only an appraiser has the proper training to value a property this way. The following are the general steps in the cost approach to determine value:

Step 1.   Estimate land value using the market approach.

Step 2.   Estimate the cost to replace the structures.

- Use industry standards (Marshall & Swift, Sweets), actual cost estimates, other square foot estimates
- Deduct depreciation
    - Curable—use a percentage based on age or actually list items worn or out-of-date
    - Incurable—elements that cannot be repaired, such as a poor design or location
- Recalculate the structure value after depreciation is deducted
- Add to land

For example, Tim needs to know the value of a fire station being abandoned by the fire department. He can't find any other properties like it that sold recently. Also, he can't estimate an income stream because he's not sure who might want the property or what it would cost them to renovate it for their individual use. He would ask his appraiser for a valuation, and the appraiser would use all three methods but may base most of the valuation on the cost approach.

The Income Approach

The **income approach** is the most common method used for income-producing property. As its name implies, the income approach is a function of income, and it can be computed in several ways.

Investment property is valued based on its income. If we know the income a property produces, we can estimate the value using one of several methods. Before we can get to the income approach, we will need to learn the following new concepts, each of which will be explained in the text below:

- Capitalization rate using the net operating income
- Net present value
- Gross rent multiplier
- Cash on cash return
- Internal rate of return (IRR)

Net operating income (NOI).   The first step in the income valuation process is to compute the net income. There are many definitions of net income, so always ask your buyer or lender what they include in their calculations. We'll do a simple calculation here and then talk about how it can vary and what to ask.

The **net operating income (NOI)** is the free and clear financial return a property generates before making any mortgage payments, paying income taxes, or taking depreciation. Let's use a small office building as an example.

Small Office Building Example

Assumptions:

Size	= 25,000 sq. ft. of leasable space (1)
Occupancy	= 85% (2)
Rent	= $20/sq. ft./yr. (represented as $/sq. ft./yr.) (3)
Operating expenses	= $7.50/sq. ft./yr. (4)
Operating reserves	= $1.50/sq. ft./yr. (5)

To calculate the NOI:

Gross possible income (GPI)	$500,000
(sq. ft. × rate; 25,000 sq. ft. × $20)	
Less: Vacancy (15%)	– 75,000
Equals: Gross Operating Income (GOI)	425,000
Less: Operating expenses	– 187,500
(sq. ft. × OE/sq. ft.; 25,000 sq. ft. × $7.50)	
Less: Operating reserves*	– 37,500
(sq. ft. × OR/sq. ft.; 25,000 sq. ft. × $1.50)	
Equals: Net operating income (NOI)	$200,000

* deduct OR if lender required

Comments:

1. Verify actual leasable square footage of the building (appraisal, et cetera).

2. Look at the market to determine the market vacancy rate and loss due to bad debt (people not paying). If the market vacancy is more than what you have on your property, an investor or banker may use the market number to be more conservative.

3. In an actual transaction, you would look at each lease. The rents will probably be different. Calculate the gross possible rent by adding up the lease amounts, factoring in any increases stated in the leases. To that you will add the "market rent" for the unleased space.

4. This is one of the hardest parts. To get operating expenses, you must look at all expenses paid by the property for its operations. This expense would include utilities, staffing, real estate taxes, insurance, janitorial, repairs, administrative costs, and management fees. You must consider all contracts currently in place and add in any services required but not shown. You need to ascertain how much it costs to operate this property. Remember that mortgage payments (called debt service), depreciation, and income taxes are not operating expenses. They are costs of owning the real estate, not operating it.

5. Lenders frequently require operating reserves to ensure that money will be available for the larger capital expenses, such as roof replacement, air conditioner equipment replacement, parking lot resurfacing, brokerage fees, tenant finish. Operating reserves are set aside each month or year to be accessed when needed.

Capital expenses, such as those noted above (such as operating reserves), are not deducted from the NOI in theory. In practice, they may be, so ask your commercial appraisers and lenders how they calculate the NOI.

Figure 6.1 | Value = NOI ÷ Cap Rate

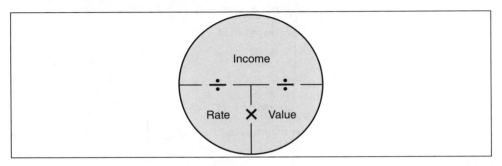

Capitalization method (using net operating income). The idea behind capitalization rate **(cap rate)** is simple. What percentage return will an investor require? Once the actual NOI is verified, then the investor can divide the NOI by their desired rate of return and that is what he or she is willing to pay. If there are other investors willing to pay more for the same property (and thereby be willing to accept a lesser rate of return), then the seller will likely sell to them. Cap rates are set by the market. An appraiser can look at similar properties recently sold and compare the sales price to the net operating incomes. That will give a range of cap rates. In other words, cap rate is the rate of return investors are receiving on similar properties.

So, if the "going cap rate" on a type of property (for example, a 90,000-square-foot shopping center with a regional grocery in a secondary market) is 9%, that means investors looking for this type of property but desiring a rate of return of more than 9% probably won't find much product because they won't be willing to pay as much as others in the market. Who will the seller sell to? All things equal, the buyer offering the best terms.

For example, let's say the NOI is $565,000, and three investors make offers. The terms are all the same; only the desired rates of return differ. To whom will the seller sell?

	Desired Rate of Return
Investor #1	8%
Investor #2	10%
Investor #3	12%

Without doing any math, we know the answer. With everything else being equal, the investor who is willing to accept the lowest return will pay more for the same property than the others. That means that Investor #1 will be the successful bidder. But how much is he or she willing to pay? And how much more is that than the others?

For this example, the math is simple (see Figure 6.1). Here is how that formula applies to our example problem.

Cap Rate Example

	Desired Rate of Return	Price Offered
Investor #1	8%	$7,062,500
		($565,000 ÷ 8%)
Investor #2	10%	$5,650,000
		($565,000 ÷ 10%)
Investor #3	12%	$4,708,333
		($565,000 ÷ 12%)

Keep in mind that if the NOI has been verified and agreed to, then all three investors are vying to buy the same income stream. If there are many investors in the market willing to accept an 8 cap rate, then the 10% and 12% investors will find little or nothing to buy when competing with them.

The 12% investor needs to find properties where the expectations are 12% returns. Typically that will be less desirable property. What makes it less desirable? The following factors are part of its undesirability problem:

■ Higher degree of risk

■ Less popular market

■ Older

■ Secondary location

■ Tenant(s) not as strong or short term leases

■ More product on the market

■ Higher vacancy

In this problem, did you notice that the sales price went down as the cap rate went up? That's an important fact to remember: As the sales price goes up, the cap rate goes down. As the sales price goes down, the cap rate goes up. The following illustration demonstrates the sales price/cap rate.

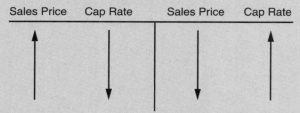

You have determined that the appropriate capitalization rate for your property is 7.8%. Data on your property is as follows:

■ Ten spaces rent for $1,000/month each.

■ One space is usually vacant.

■ Expenses run $450/space/month that you pay whether vacant or occupied.

■ Reserves run $25/space/month.

1. Compute the adjusted NOI (after deducting reserves).

2. Compute the value using the cap rate given.

Solution:

Income:

10 spaces × $1,000 × 12 months =	$120,000
Less vacancy: 1 space × $1,000 × 12 months	− 12,000
Total income	$108,000

Expenses:

10 spaces × $450 × 12 months =	− 54,000
Net operating income	$54,000

Less reserves:

10 spaces × $25 × 12 months	− 3,000
Adjusted NOI	$51,000

$51,000 ÷ 7.8% = $653,846 = Property value

Creating a pro forma. Let's concentrate on the other side of the equation for a moment: the **operating expenses**. We will look at an existing property and create a three-year operating pro forma.

Estimating Income

Let's start with an existing office building. A prospective buyer will investigate the income, primarily rent from leases, expected rent increases, losses due to expected move outs, and income from leasing any vacant space. Expenses can be estimated by reviewing the existing contracts and the property's history and then forecasting any increases or savings in the future.

The following is what we know:

- Leasable square footage: 45,000

Tenant leases:

Suite	Square Feet	Rent/Square Foot	Annual Rent	Lease Expiration
101	5,000	$20	$100,000	8 more yrs.
102	5,000	18	90,000	3 more yrs.
103	2,500	0	0	Vacant
104	2,500	22	55,000	5 yrs.
201	7,500	15	112,500	within 1 yr.
204	7,500	17.50	131,250	2 yrs.
300	15,000	16	240,000	2 yrs.
Total	45,000		$728,750	

Expenses:

Operating expenses:

Utilities	$75,000
Management	35,000
Administrative	15,000
Salaries	50,000
Maintenance	65,000
Grounds	48,000
Insurance	27,000
Miscellaneous	15,000
Real estate taxes	30,000
Total	$360,000
Less: Reserves	– 30,000 (if required by the lender)
Net operating income	$338,750, let's call it $340,000

($728,750 – $360,000 – $30,000 = $338,750)

In addition, you feel that the vacant space will be leased by the end of the year. When it does get leased, you expect to get rent of $22 per square foot, pay a broker's fee of $10,000, and pay some tenant improvement costs of $65,000.

You hope you can reduce some of the operating expenses through better contract negotiation but feel that will be offset by increases in taxes and utilities.

The figures and assumptions above have taken someone substantial time to assemble, compile, and analyze.

Using the different income valuation methods listed earlier, we will now go on to look at how an investor might view this property using the capitalization approach.

Note that an actual investor or a commercial appraiser will go into much more depth and analysis than we will see here. This exercise should just acquaint you with the basics.

Using the Capitalization Rate

Let's use the capitalization rate to estimate the value of this property.

Assumptions: NOI = $340,000 in year 1
Market Cap Rate = 11%
NOI ÷ Cap rate = Value
$340,000 ÷ 11% = $3,090,909

However, there is income expected in year 2 but also some expense for tenant improvements and broker's fees.

Year 2 NOI might look like:

Income:	$728,750 + $55,000 = $783,750
Expenses:	– 360,000
Reserves:	– 30,000
Brokers fee*:	– 10,000
Tenant improvements*:	– 65,000
Money left (NOI)	$318,750

Value using year 2:
$318,750 ÷ 11% = $2,897,728, or nearly $200,000 less than year 1.
*The broker's fee and tenant improvements will be amortized and not taken as an expense in year 2. However the checks will have to be written, and the money will be spent in year 2, regardless of the tax treatment.

Let's look at year 3, then.

Income: $783,750
Expenses: – 360,000
Reserves: – 30,000 (if required by lender)
NOI $393,750

$393,750 ÷ 11% = $3,579,545

So, you have the following:
Year 1 $3,090,909
Year 2 $2,897,728
Year 3 $3,579,545

Depending on how long the investor plans to hold the property and tax considerations, the investor will pay somewhere in between these numbers. There are very sophisticated methods of reconciling these. Averaging is not appropriate because it assumes that each year has the same impact. Cash flow from year 1 is worth more than cash flow from year 3. The internal rate of return would be one method an investor might use to decide on final asking price. To use it, we would have to know the financing arrangements, the discount rate, the down payment, and the closing costs.

There are other ways to use the income to make buying and selling decisions. For example, if investors know their desired return and they know how much cash the property generates, they can compute an offering price. One way to do this is by computing the net present value of an investment.

Net present value.   The **net present value (NPV)** discounts all cash flows back to the present value using a stated discount rate (investor's yield) and offsets those cash flows against the initial investment to show the net value of an investment today. A positive NPV means that the investment will achieve more than the discount rate (now better referred to as *yield*) or that the investors could pay "that much more" for the property and still achieve their stated rate. A negative NPV means just the opposite—investors who will not achieve desired yield or to achieve desired yield must pay that amount less. An NPV of zero means that the investors will achieve the desired yield given the down payment and cash flows shown.

Note that the following examples assume use of a financial calculator. In these cases, the Hewlett-Packard 10bII is used and keystrokes are shown. Financial calculators are not difficult to master, but the beginner should start to learn to use them with a specialized class or book. There are other calculators and financial programs available. Use the one which best suits your needs by asking others in your area for recommendations.

Gross rent multiplier.   Another way to decide on an asking price is to compare the return on the rent on other similar investments. The **gross rent multiplier (GRM)** is a method used. The math is simple and explained below. We will use GRM to stand for gross rent multiplier and SP to stand for sales price. Multifamily properties use this method (in addition to others) more than other types of property.

Net Present Value

- Down payment is $10,000 (Remember that this will be a negative number when entered into the calculator.)

- Cash flows for the next four years are: $0; $1,000; $5,000; $7,931

- Desired discount rate (yield) = 7%

- Be sure P/YR is set to 1 (One compounding period per year)

- Key in ($10,000) to Cfo

- Key in cash flows individually, in order, using CFj key

- Key in desired discount rate, 7, using I/YR key

- Solve for NPV by hitting SHIFT and NPV

In this example, NPV = +$1,005. This means that the investor will do better than a 7% yield, or that the investor could pay up to $1,005 more for the property and still achieve a 7% yield.

Do the same problem but with discount rate/yield of 13 instead of 7.

NPV = –$887. This means that the investor will not achieve a 13% yield, or, that in order to do so, he or she must pay $887 less up front.

What to pay?

Do the same problem, but this time the down payment is unknown. The debt is known, and mortgage payments are factored into cash flows. What we don't know is how much we need to put down (remember that down payment + debt = sales price).

- CFo = 0 (Because we don't know down payment)

- Key in cash flows in order using CFj key.

- Enter desired yield using I/YR key (let's use 10%, but we will key in just 10; the key will make it a %).

- Solve for NPV by hitting SHIFT and NPV.

NPV = $10,000, which is what an investor would put down and still receive a 10% return (yield).

To arrive at a gross rent multiplier, first find market comparables, then divide their sales price by their actual gross rental income (before any expenses). The income can be monthly or annual income, as long as you are consistent throughout the problem.

Example:

Comp's SP = $150,000, Rent = 15,000/yr., GRM = 10 ($150,000 ÷ $15,000 = 10)

To derive value using the gross rent multiplier method, take the subject property's potential rental income multiplied by the GRM (potential rental income × GRM = investment value).

Sometimes an investor will have specific GRM standards. For example, a given investor might always buy properties at 8.5 times their rent. In that case, just take the subject property's potential rental income multiplied by the investor's GRM to arrive at what the investor would pay.

> Property's annual potential income is $100,000
>
> Investor's GRM is 8
>
> $100,000 × 8 = $800,000 (what investor is likely to pay)

The GRM method may seem too simple, and, in fact, there are several disadvantages in using it. Vacancy, collection losses, expenses, financing, and tax issues are not taken into account, which could provide a skewed notion of a property's value.

Cash on cash return.   Sometimes investors merely want to compare the return they can receive from their initial cash outlay to other investment opportunities.

To find the **cash on cash return**, look at the first year's cash flow (before taxes) of the subject property. Divide the cash flow proceeds by the initial cash investment (which would include the down payment and sometimes closing costs) to get cash on cash return.

Cash on Cash Return

Say a property was for sale with a $500,000 mortgage. The investor comes to the table with a cash on cash requirement of 10%. Cash flow before taxes (CFBT) is $20,000. The investor would be willing to pay the following:

$20,000 ÷ 10% = $200,000 (down payment)
                 $500,000 (mortgage)
Total value $700,000

Let's try finding the cash on cash return, given the price asked, amount financed, and annual CFBT.

Price asked: $840,000
Amt. financed $620,000
Down payment required $220,000
Estimated annual CFBT = $25,000 (cash money)

Cash on cash return = $25,000 ÷ $220,000 = 11.36%

So, our sample investor invested $220,000, and gets back $25,000 per year.

Now the investor can decide if he or she could get a better return on the $220,000 elsewhere—stocks, bonds, CDs, collectibles, gold, futures, et cetera.

The disadvantage of the cash on cash return valuation method is that it does not consider tax impact, and it looks at one year only. The $25,000 CFBT that we found may be the best year ever or the worst. A more thorough method to analyze cash returns is to use the internal rate of return.

Internal rate of return.   The **internal rate of return (IRR)** takes into account the time and value of money on an investment and measures the return on the investment.

The things to consider are: When the money is put in, how long it stays in investment, how much comes out and when, and what the sales proceeds are. This analysis can be done before tax or after tax.

Internal Rate of Return

The property requires a down payment of $20,000. It produces a cash flow of $3,000 per year. The holding period is five years. It's estimated that at the end of five years there will be a $24,000 profit from the sales proceeds.

- Using your financial calculator, key in the initial investment of ($20,000) for year 0 (note that it is a negative number, as it is money going out).

- Key in $3,000 and press pmt key (you are getting a payment of $3,000).

- Key in number of payments—holding period (n = 5).

- Solve for i (interest) to give the IRR.

- IRR = 17.81%

Now if cash flows are different amounts, you must use the Cfo and CFj keys and the IRR key.

Initial investment (down payment) = $10,000; cash flows are: $0; $1,000; $5,000; $7,931. What is the IRR?

- Cfo = ($10,000)

- CFj = 0

- CFj = $1,000

- CFj = $5,000

- CFj = $7,931

- Shift IRR = 10%

Note that if the property were sold at the end of year 4, add proceeds (profit) to year 4 CF before keying in.

We've looked at a number of ways a buyer (or seller) may view the financial aspects of a property. Which one to use? It depends on the investors' goals and other investment opportunities. Investors may use all the methods described above.

■ Additional Valuation Topics

Cash Flow

Instead of NOI, some return calculations use **cash flow**. NOI is typically used because "the NOI is what the NOI is." Given known market conditions in conjunction with executed leases, the income can be determined. Once all service contracts are reviewed and past expenses analyzed, operating expenses can be determined. Subtract operating expenses from adjusted income and you get the NOI. Regardless of who does the calculations, the market and contracts in place determine income and expenses. Cash flow is what is left after paying the mortgage payment. Because the terms of a loan may depend on the borrower's credit and relationship with a lender, it is difficult for a broker to calculate cash flow other than to use market figures. Some buyers may find more favorable financing and some may not.

Let's use the earlier office building example and assume that the market for financing for credit borrowers is as follows:

Cash Flow

■ 75% loan to value (LTV)

■ Interest rate = 6%

■ Payment schedule = 25 years

There will be costs to borrow the funds that would be treated as an acquisition expense and not affect the NOI, but for simplicity we will ignore those for now.

Let's say that the lender has decided to use a blended value of $3,100,000.

Loan = $3,100,000 × 75% = $2,325,000

Annual debt service (D/S) = $180,000 (interest + principal) (using a financial calculator)

Cash flow would be:

	Year 1	Year 2	Year 3
NOI	$340,000	$318,750	$393,750
D/S	−180,000	−180,000	−180,000
CFBT*	$160,000	$138,750	$213,750

*CFBT = cash flow before depreciation, amortization, and taxes

Depreciation and amortization are noncash items but affect the taxable income and hence the taxes on income due.

Residual Value

When looking at the return over the life of the investment, a disposition value will have to be calculated. This is where investors look into their crystal ball to determine appreciation. If we assume that a property is worth what its income stream is worth, then we will merely need to run the income and expense numbers out through the holding period, estimate a cap rate, and calculate the expected sales price.

From there we can estimate closing costs to determine total return over the ownership period, both before and after taxes. But what if it's land without improvements?

Valuing Land

As explained in Chapter 4, land can be valued using the market or income approach. To value land on the income approach, one must determine how much value the land brings to the overall value of the development. This is a complex process and is best left to an experienced land broker or a commercial appraiser. To use the market approach, one must gather all the information listed below. The steps are simple but can be time-consuming.

Step 1. Gather all relevant data on the subject property. We must know its size, shape, zoning, and so on, so we can select sold properties to compare it to those that are truly comparable.

Step 2. Create a profile sheet on the subject property listing the features described earlier.

Step 3. Take photos of the property from as many angles as possible. If the site is large, aerial photos might be necessary.

Step 4. Take photos of the surrounding area.

Step 5. Gather any reports, surveys, and so on that the owner has.

Step 6. Walk the site to gain familiarity. Whoever buys it will do so, and no surprises is a good thing! Be careful: Never go alone, especially if it is remote or a large site. Dress properly for a site walk; take your camera and some protection, such as a walking stick; and make sure your cell phone is charged. Let someone know where you are going.

Step 7. Find out any history about the site. A local longtime property owner is an excellent source for history. If that is not a choice, then a longtime local resident can probably tell an agent about the property. This might be another agent, an attorney, a neighbor, et cetera. For example, a developer bought a piece of land without asking questions about its history and found out during construction that there were soil problems. When one of the locals heard about this, he said he wasn't surprised because part of the site used to be underwater! That would have been helpful for the developer to know.

Step 8. Select recently sold comparables (comps). This is one of the most important steps because the sites need to be comparable! Many owners believe that their property is worth more than it is because they heard that another piece of property, similar to theirs, they think, sold for a very high price. The fact may be that the other property is on the main highway with a lot of frontage and exposure, and their property has no important frontage, is partially in the floodplain, and has severe topography.

Step 9. Once the comps are selected, the agent must discover as much about the sales as possible. Was owner financing used? Were there any unusual provisions in the sales contract?

Where does the agent get this information? This is indeed the hard part. If land sales are routinely handled through a multiple listing service (MLS) or a commercial information exchange (CIE), the agent may be able to pull up most of what is needed through those services if the agent has access to them as a member or subscriber. If land is not typically shown in the MLS or CIE, then the agent must rely on other resources.

Any land broker needs to know the other land brokers in the area, bankers who finance land sales, and appraisers who work on land deals. Additional sources of information are the developers who buy raw land and the engineers and architects who work with developers.

Step 10. Once the facts about the recently sold comparables are known, the agent can look to see what other tracts of comparable land are on the market. In other words, who will be competing for the same buyers? Knowing who will be competing can help the agent determine an asking price.

Step 11. Run it up the flagpole, which means, try putting the property on the market with the price you have set. In emerging markets, it is difficult to find a comfort level with pricing. If several offers come in early, it is probably priced too low. If no offers come in for a long period of time, it is probably priced too high.

Using the income approach (which is covered in detail in this chapter), a broker can estimate the value of a completed project then back out the improvements to get an idea of how much the land contributes.

For example, using the income approach, a broker/developer estimates that a development is worth $5,000,000. The actual cost of development excluding land, interest carry on the land, and site improvements is estimated to be $3,750,000. That means that the balance ($5,000,000 – $3,750,000 = $1,250,000) is available for land, site improvements, interest carry, and profit.

This method compares apples and oranges because the value is based on the income produced, and the land value is computed on the cost approach. But when a developer is looking at land, they estimate how much they can pay for the land based on the eventual value of the completed project. Another problem with using this approach is that income is based on the tenants' rents and the strength of the tenants (which is reflected in the capitalization rates), and until the tenants are secured, the value may be uncertain.

■ Additional Resources

One of the best resources for information about understanding the financial aspects of income properties is the CCIM Institute (www.ccim.com). Recognized for its preeminence within the industry, the CCIM curriculum represents the core knowledge expected of commercial investment practitioners, regardless of the diversity of specializations within the industry. The CCIM curriculum consists of four core courses that incorporate the essential CCIM skill sets: financial analysis, market analysis, user decision analysis, and investment analysis for commercial investment real estate. Additional curriculum requirements may be completed through CCIM elective courses, transfer credit for graduate education or professional recognition, and qualifying non-CCIM education.

Following the course work, candidates must submit a résumé of closed transactions or consultations, or both, showing a depth of experience in the commercial investment field. After fulfilling these requirements, candidates must successfully complete a comprehensive examination to earn the CCIM designation. This designation process ensures that CCIMs are proficient not only in theory but also in practice.

| case study | **Shopping Center** |

Start with the following assumptions:

- Small shopping center
- Seven spaces, each 1,000 square feet
- Six rented at $20 per square foot
- Expenses are $1.50 per square foot, which is passed through to the tenants
- "Going cap rate" for this type of center today is 8%

We are going to disregard any reserves or capital expenses for the purposes of this exercise.

1. How much rent will you receive?

   ~~110,000~~   120,000

2. How much of the expenses are paid by the owner?

   ~~$0~~   -$1,500

3. What is the NOI?

   ~~$128,750~~   · ~~$109,500~~ $118,500

4. With the 8% cap rate, what would a typical investor pay?

   ~~$1,609,750 375~~   ~~$1,368,150~~ $1,481,250.

5. If the last space were rented, how much more would the likely selling price of the center?

   ~~$1,609,375~~ $268,750

■ Review Questions

1. Which is the *MOST* common method used to analyze and value investment property?
   a. Sales comparison approach
   b. Cost approach
   c. Income approach
   d. Any of these

2. The sales comparison approach can be used
   a. in every analysis.
   b. only when there are enough current comparables.
   c. only when income is low.
   d. only in connection with another method, such as the cost approach.

3. A property has total monthly income of $20,000 and total monthly operating expenses of $7,500. Ignoring any deductions for reserves, what is the property's annual NOI?
   a. $12,500
   b. $27,500
   c. $150,000
   d. $200,000

4. Using the information from question 3, if the capitalization rate is 8%, what is the value?
   a. $100,000
   b. $156,250
   c. $1,875,000
   d. $3,000,000

5. Which of the following would *NOT* be considered an operating expense?
   a. Interest expense (on the mortgage)
   b. Utility expenses
   c. Real estate taxes
   d. Common area maintenance

7 Finance

overview

It might seem strange for a commercial real estate primer to include a chapter on real estate finance. After all, if you wanted to work in the financial area, you'd work for a bank, right? But consider what you will need to know to be successful in the commercial real estate field. If a property is going to be difficult to finance, then it stands to reason that it may be more difficult to sell—there will be fewer buyers. Fewer buyers may lessen the value. If a broker understands the basics of finance, the broker can estimate the value and desirability of a property. ■

learning objectives

When you have completed this chapter, you will be able to

■ describe the differences between commercial and residential loans,

■ list different lender types for commercial loans, and

■ describe financing alternatives.

■ Key Terms

conduit

commercial mortgage backed securities (CMBS)

debt service coverage ratio (DSCR)

deed of trust

exculpated loan

LIBOR

limited liability company (LLC)

limited partnership

mortgage

mortgage broker

real estate investment trust (REIT)

underwriting

■ The Commercial Finance Market

A major component of commercial real estate brokerage is the ability to finance the property. If lenders will lend, builders will build. Very few, if any, developers self-finance their developments. While interest rates remain relatively low, using someone else's money to build remains attractive. Along with this easy money, however, comes the downside of overbuilding.

When a new real estate product is successful (such as starter homes, drugstores, and miniwarehouses), those first in the market may have had to blaze the path. The next group in the market may reap some of the reward, but eventually too many will enter the arena with poorly thought-out concepts and flood the market with product—some good, some terrible. The weakest competitors, sometimes referred to as *weak sisters*, will go away. However, what remains is too much product and wary lenders.

A little competition is a good thing; too much can crush a market. And the market can take years to recover.

Commercial Lenders

Lenders have two goals: first, to get their money back, and get the loan fully repaid, and second, to make a profit on the money.

Lenders have a difficult job because they must both minimize risk and be aggressive. After suffering through an overbuilt market, they may be wary for a period of time. The quotes on loans may be less attractive or not forthcoming at all. On the other hand, as soon as there is a surplus of money to lend, loans become very easy to obtain. It's simply the law of supply and demand.

Commercial real estate lenders are different from residential real estate lenders. Most residential loans are quickly sold into the secondary market to investors such as Fannie Mae or Freddie Mac. The secondary-market sales allow cash to flow back to the lender to loan to other borrowers.

Sales to Fannie Mae and Freddie Mac are not as common in commercial real estate. Since the early 1990s, it has become more popular to package loans and sell them to investors (commonly referred to as *conduits*). But since commercial loans are harder to make in a uniform manner, it is harder to bundle loans for sale into the secondary market. There are so few standard deals in commercial real estate.

Because lenders then must hold the loan in their own portfolio until payoff, there is more scrutiny over the securitization. In other words, what makes the loan a low risk? And if the lenders were to foreclose, is it likely that they could get their money back?

Some lenders have **mortgage brokers** (sometimes referred to as *correspondents*) arrange their loans, while others have staff within their organization represent them. As a real estate broker brings buyers and sellers together for a fee, a mortgage broker or mortgage banker brings a borrower and lender together for a fee. Typically the fee is paid by the borrower, and the mortgage banker or mortgage broker represents the lender—just as in residential real estate.

In any case, any borrower should ask a lender, or the lender's representative, what is most important to that lender and what terms the lender is currently offering.

A lender who has financed several apartment developments for a developer may suddenly find that they have no more funds to put out in the real estate lending area for apartments. Their apartment portfolio is full, and they will not be making any more loans on that product in the near future. This can substantially alter a developer's plans. The developer may have proceeded assuming that this lender would have the funds available. He or she may even have designed the project to meet the lender's preferences only to find that another lender has other preferences, or worse, that no one is in the market right now to lend money on that product.

What Do Lenders Look for in Potential Borrowers?

Let's begin our look at the financing process from the lenders' point of view. Their two goals are to profit on the loan and to get their money back without having to foreclose. What qualities would make the lender most comfortable with a loan prospect? To ascertain those qualities, ask the following questions:

- Does the developer have experience with this type of project?

- Does the developer have other sources of money? If the project starts to falter, does the developer have money to carry them through, or will the developer just turn everything over to the lender?

- Is the developer's project in their area? Building where one has experience or has built other projects is helpful. Besides knowing the area and what is happening in the economy, the developer has personal ties with the area, officials, and others. This would make the developer motivated to keep the project going and make a success of it.

- Have tenants been secured? Who are they? Has the developer worked with them before? This is one of the most important questions. The value of income property is the ability of the property to produce consistent income. The better the tenant, the more consistent the income.

- What is the developer's history with working with lenders? Is he or she flexible? Does he or she keep his or her word?

- Is this project risky? Is it the first one of its kind or an experiment? Is it the last one in an already overbuilt market?

- How much of his or her own money is the developer putting into this project? The more equity a developer has in a project, the less likely he or she is to walk away easily.

- Does the developer have other partners in this development? This can be a plus or a minus depending on who the partners are and how much participation they will have.

- How many other projects does the developer have going on? Someone spread too thin is more likely to fail. The lender doesn't want to take on this kind of risk.

- What is the developer's financial condition? Even if the loan will not require personal guarantees, the better off financially the developer is, the more comfortable the lender is.

- What is happening in the market? Is the area growing, losing jobs, dramatically changing its base? How will this development fare?

What if the borrower is not a developer, but an investor looking to buy investment property? What would a lender look at here?

Overall, the traits are the same for investors and developers, but there are a few additional points to consider. Do the investors know their trade? What is their track record? How financially fit are they? Can they weather a downturn in the market? Are their tenants stable and strong?

With all the emphasis lenders place on experience, how would a first-time developer or investor ever get started? Obviously a first-timer is riskier than a seasoned pro, but remember that the loan will be secured by the real estate. So if the real estate makes sense, then the lender may feel like taking that risk. Lenders may not offer the same terms to the newcomer as they would on a similar deal with a seasoned pro, but at least the newcomer has gotten a start in the business. Remember that risk is the most important factor. The riskier a transaction is, the more it will cost. The less risky it is, the more attractive terms a developer can expect. When there is excess money to "put out" (lend), lenders may be competing for a developer's or investor's business.

Most lenders specialize in certain products. The larger the lender, the more diversified their portfolio. The lender who just financed a $27 million apartment complex may not be interested in financing a $4 million Walgreen's or even a multimillion-dollar Walmart. On the other hand, a smaller lender may only finance certain types within their price range. At some point, any lender may decide to diversify. Because they have only so much money they can lend on real estate loans, they may choose to try a different product. In order to spread the risk, the lender should have a broad range of real estate loans. If lenders had all of their real estate loans placed on Enron office buildings, for example, they would have taken a substantial hit when Enron fell on hard times.

■ Types of Lenders

When we think of borrowing money, we may think of the bank where we do business or where we have our checking account. In commercial real estate, there are many different types of lenders with different requirements and goals. Let's look at some below.

Commercial Banks

This category of lender includes Chase, Bank of America, Wells Fargo, and Citibank, as well as smaller regional banks or private banks.

Commercial banks may provide some mortgage loans, but they are better suited for short-term loans, such as bridge or construction loans. The amount that a lender can place in loans is dependent on their deposits and the activity of those deposits. Long-term loans tie up money for long periods of time unless a lender sells the loan to other investors or lenders. A lender may work with other lenders when making loans and act as a mortgage broker, collecting a fee, and perhaps being able to service the loan.

Commercial banks have become more aggressive in making long-term commercial real estate loans, and, depending on the amount of money they have to invest in loans, they may be the best place for a new developer or investor to start when looking for financing.

Savings Associations

Savings associations, or thrifts, can be state or federally chartered. They used to be called savings and loans and were at one time the primary source for residential and small commercial real estate loans. After the Tax Reform Act of 1986 and the fallout from underperforming loans, about 35% of savings and loans closed. Those remaining had some problem loans and became more selective in future loans made. Now called savings associations, they still make many mortgage loans but are not the market force they were years ago. Nevertheless, if a developer or investor has a relationship with a savings association, that might be the best place to start looking for financing. Some savings associations are quite aggressive in making commercial real estate loans, but their funds are limited.

Insurance Companies

These financiers include companies such as MetLife and Nationwide, and they are referred to as *life companies*. They have funds (accumulated through premiums paid for insurance policies) to invest and typically finance larger projects that are considered *institutional-grade* or *investment-quality* developments. These properties are in major markets and are of the size and quality that an institutional investor would seek. Life companies have specific preferences in the products they finance. To minimize risk, they like to finance properties they understand and have a comfort level with. They especially like to finance property types that they have financed before.

They typically work through a correspondent—a mortgage broker or mortgage banker—who knows their criteria. The borrower pays the fee to the broker or banker, but the broker or banker represents the lender, the life company.

Once a relationship is formed between a life company and a developer/investor, the life company may act as the developer's main or lead lender in future developments. Remember that, at some point, the lender may loan all they want or can on a certain product type so funds may become scarce for a period of time and the developer will have to seek money elsewhere.

The smaller life companies may be niche lenders and have funds available for unusual projects or those in unusual locations. They may work through mortgage bankers or brokers or have their own staff handle the loans.

Pension Funds

Another source for institutional-grade loans are pension funds. The pension fund advisors seek to maximize the return and minimize the risk because they are dealing with employees' retirement monies.

They operate much like the life companies and can work through mortgage bankers and mortgage brokers or through their own staff.

An interesting part of the market comes to light when dealing with both pension funds and REITs (discussed next). Like investors, lenders can find themselves guilty of the "herd mentality." This happens when large groups of lenders compete for certain product types (say neighborhood, grocery anchored–shopping centers, or Class A apartments). When there is too much money available for a certain product type, it encourages developers to build that product even if there is little or no need for it. After all, the lender will lend money. Because many of the larger pension funds take their cue from Wall Street when it comes to product types and rates, a hiccup in the market can create havoc.

Real Estate Investment Trusts (REITs)

Real estate investment trusts (REITs) started to become more popular in the 1970s, and since that time additional REIT regulations have been enacted to protect investors. There are two types of REITs—equity REITs and mortgage REITs. These can be public or private.

Equity REITs are portfolios of investment-grade income-producing properties. Typically one type of property—such as apartments, neighborhood shopping centers, office buildings, or industrial properties—makes up the portfolio.

Investors buy shares of the portfolios, much like stock. They enjoy the income and tax benefits of their investment, assuming the portfolio does well. For a REIT to be successful, the following things must occur:

- The properties must be successful.
- The properties must have been purchased at the right price.
- The debt on the properties must be low (under 40%).
- The properties must be well managed.
- The REIT must be well managed.
- The REIT must continue to grow.
- The properties must be sold at the right time.
- The overall financial market must be stable.
- Major investors must have confidence in the REIT.

Like anything else, a product type can become overbuilt and fall out of favor. If the REIT is comprised of that product type, then the REIT's ability to sell any of their properties at an attractive price is hampered.

Mortgage REITs are made up of groups of similar mortgages on similar properties. Investors buy shares of this mortgage portfolio and enjoy returns based on the quality of the loans in the REIT and the repayment of those loans.

Interest rates and the money market influence the success of mortgage REITs. If the REIT is comprised of higher interest loans and the interest rates drop, then it's expected that some of the loans will be refinanced and no longer be part of the portfolio, or if they are, will be producing a lower return than before.

Mortgage REITs fall in and out of popularity depending on alternative revenue sources available to borrowers and investment opportunities available to the REIT investors. Equity REITs have been around for 30 years and also change according to the fluctuation of the investment market.

A REIT can make money available using its own personnel or may use mortgage bankers and mortgage brokers in the same way as life companies and pension funds.

Private Funds

There are always groups of private investors who provide mortgage or equity money to developers and investors. A financial advisor can arrange for a developer to meet with these groups as can another lender. Private investors can also be found through personal relationships.

Government

There may be tax incentives or tax abatements involved in government loans. For projects that benefit an area or municipality, there may be government mortgage or acquisition monies available with attractive terms. These monies may be available from a district, city, county, state, or the U.S. government.

An example is the use of tax increment financing (TIF). Every state (except Arizona as of 2005) has some form of TIF. The program differs depending on the state, but TIF is a way for the government to provide funds for development in targeted areas, stimulate building, and improve neighborhoods. For example, let's say there is a blighted area outside of the central business district (CBD). Developers are interested in developing in the area, but the area needs massive work on its infrastructure, including roads, parking, utilities, parks, et cetera. No developer is willing to take on all of that infrastructure repair, but if the city or county could help out, then the developer would be willing to take a risk. Most cities or counties don't have surplus funds to handle this, so they may turn to TIF. The municipality will define a geographic area. The tax base of that area will be recognized. The municipality will offer bonds to raise money for the infrastructure, and the bonds will be repaid by the increased taxes (over the starting base) over time. While TIF is a valuable tool for governments, because they can use increased value to fund improvements, there are a couple of downsides to TIF. The quality of the bonds depends on the credit of the city or county. If the city or county is overextended or has poor credit, then the bonds may not be sufficient. If the project isn't successful, then the bonds will have to be repaid through other means.

Summary of Lenders

With any type of loan, it is important to understand where a lender's funds originate. Banks and savings associations use a portion of depositors' money, and monies from other profit centers of the bank. For example, a bank may be managing a trust fund for a client and may choose to invest in a low-risk mortgage. Typically long-term loans need to come from long-term funds on hand, not short-term, or demand accounts. Short-term monies are best suited to short-term loans, such as construction loans or acquisition loans.

Sometimes the lenders originate their own loans, and sometimes they turn to mortgage bankers or mortgage brokers. Remember, as a real estate broker brings buyers and sellers together for a fee, a mortgage broker or mortgage banker brings a borrower and lender together for a fee. Typically the fee is paid by the borrower and the mortgage banker or mortgage broker represents the lender—just as in residential real estate. The fees vary and are negotiable. A mortgage banker or mortgage broker who represents a lender may be referred to as their correspondent.

There are also other sources for loans, less used in commercial real estate, such as credit unions and private loan companies. They have their niche and should be considered if available.

■ Types of Loans

Let's look at the different types of real estate financing, who would offer them, and some special characteristics of each.

Mortgage Loan, Long-Term

A long-term mortgage loan is the permanent mortgage loan. The typical long-term mortgage loan is for 10, 15, or 20 years or more and amortizes. For those with a term less than 25 years, there may be a balloon at the end. Even though a loan may have a 15-year term, the schedule (how the payments are computed) may be longer, say 25 years. Therefore, at the end of the term, there still is a balance due because the payments acted as if the loan was for a longer period of time. A car lease works on the same principal.

These loans can be recourse or nonrecourse. *Recourse loans* mean that the lender has recourse for debt recovery in addition to the real estate. In other words, in case of default, the lender can take the property and something else. What else? A recourse loan requires the borrower to make a personal guarantee to the lender to repay the loan. Therefore the borrower's other assets are available. A borrower would prefer to have only the subject property as collateral and not have to offer any personal guarantees. This would be a nonrecourse loan. Another term used is **exculpated loan**. In the case of a nonrecourse loan, the lender needs to ensure that the value of the real estate is more than sufficient to secure the loan because that is all the security they have!

Life companies, mortgage companies, pension funds, and banks make these long-term mortgage loans.

Acquisition Loan

This is usually a short-term interest-only loan made by a bank or savings association to a borrower they know. For collateral, the lender will want a personal guarantee from the borrower and perhaps the real estate as additional security. For example, investors plan to buy a tract of land to develop that they will finance with a construction loan when they get all their numbers and contract together. Meanwhile, they must close on the land. They may use an acquisition loan to buy the land. If their construction loan is with the same lender, the lender may roll the acquisition loan into the construction loan when the time comes.

Bridge Loan

This is a loan, typically a short-term and interest-only loan, that provides a borrower sometime between two other loans. For example, let's say that the borrower is refinancing a property and must pay off the original loan by August 31. The borrower is in the process of arranging for a new permanent long-term mortgage loan but will not be able to close it until October 15. A 45-day bridge loan may be the solution.

Construction Loan

This is a short-term interest-only loan made to finance the construction of a project. This loan has the real estate and improvements as security for the debt plus the personal guarantee of the borrower. Most lenders will require the borrower to have some equity in the project so that the lender is not financing the entire construction expense.

Because these loans are designed to be short-term loans, the lender may require that the borrower have a permanent loan in place (a takeout) at some point during the construction period. Otherwise a construction lender may find that they are acting as a temporary permanent lender. Remember that lenders lend what they have, and having to work long term with a borrower with short-term money can be a problem for a lender.

A Note on Interest Rates

The interest rate on an interest-only loan can be tied to any number of indexes. The most common indexes are the prime rate (the rate charged to a lender's best customers), the London InterBank Offering Rate or **LIBOR**, and U.S. Treasury bonds. There are many other indexes, but these are the most common for real estate loans at this time. The interest rate to be paid is quoted on index plus additional basis points. There are 100 basis points in 1%. Therefore, 50 BP = 0.5%.

So, if 30-day LIBOR is 3.65 and the rate quoted is 30-day LIBOR + 180 BP, what is the interest rate? Answer: 3.65 + 1.80 = 5.45%.

It is not enough to say LIBOR; you need to specify the term—30 days, 60 days, 6 months, and so on. The term used depends on the market and the property being financed. The same is true for bonds. The prime rate, however, is the same rate no matter what the terms.

It is also important how interest is charged. Most loans use compounded interest. That ends up meaning that interest is charged on interest during the period. Later on we will look at the life of a construction loan and how the interest is calculated.

Mini-Perm Loan

A *mini-perm loan* is a combination construction and short-term permanent loan. This loan is most frequently used when the developer plans to sell the property soon after construction or when permanent loans are difficult to get in advance.

The construction part is handled like any construction loan. At some point (usually when the project is complete and has its certificate of occupancy or is certified by the project architect) the loan may turn into an amortizing loan that has portions being paid toward interest and principal. The loan may also stay as an interest-only one.

If the loan amortizes, then it has a balloon payment at the end of the term. If it is an interest-only loan, then the loan principal is due at the end of the term.

Junior Loan

A *junior loan* is any loan that does not have first-lien position. A loan may start out as a senior (or only) loan but change positions through a subordination agreement.

Let's say that an owner did extensive renovations to an office building and borrowed money to do this. The intention is to repay the debt with increased rent from the tenant. This loan is secondary to the mortgage loan. Rates decrease and the owner decides to refinance the mortgage loan but leaves the renovation loan in place. Once the first mortgage loan is repaid, the renovation loan will move to first place. Because the new mortgage lender will not accept a secondary position, it will execute a subordination agreement with the renovation loan lender to allow the mortgage lender to take first place. A couple of types of junior loans are described below—equity loan and mezzanine loan.

Equity loan. An *equity loan* is used to fund some or all of the equity needed on a project. The equity is the difference between the value and the loan. In a new development, equity is the difference between the total cost and the mortgage loan.

As in mezzanine financing, the equity is riskier and has a higher rate. The equity lender has a secondary position and may receive a portion of the appreciation in addition to the interest rate.

Equity loans used to be handled through syndications, which are discussed later in this chapter. Now, there are sources for equity loans similar to those for mezzanine financing.

Mezzanine loan.   The *mezzanine loan* provides cash to the developer to pay for the project. For example, let's say the cost to build a development is $20 million. The permanent loan will provide $15 million, and the developer has $2 million of his own money to put in the project. That leaves a shortfall of $3 million. The developer expects to sell some outparcels (tracts adjoining the development that could be used by retailers, banks, restaurants, etc.) in the next two to three years as the project matures, and, therefore, could repay the $3 million at that time. In the meantime, he needs $3 million to be able to build the project.

A bank or private investor would be the most common source of these mezzanine funds, and the interest rate charged would reflect the higher level of risk. In fact, the rate may be a combination of interest rate and a portion of the profit when the outparcels are sold.

This type of financing is short term and pricey and can be structured a number of ways. Sometimes this is lumped onto the creative financing category. The mezzanine lender takes a secondary position when it comes to liens. The general rule of thumb is that the permanent mortgage comes first and is referred to as the senior loan. All others are junior loans.

Wraparound Loan

Often referred to as a *wrap*, this type of loan "wraps around" and includes an existing loan to create the new, larger loan.

For example, let's say that there is a $2 million loan on a property with 10 years left on its term. Let's also say that there is no due-on-sale clause. A due-on-sale clause means that the loan is due when the property is sold; the loan cannot be transferred with the sale. A buyer agrees to buy the property for $3.5 million and the seller agrees to 100% financing with a wrap.

Here's what happens: The seller is wrapping his $1.5 million seller financing around the existing $2 million loan to make a total loan of $3.5 million. The buyer would make payments on the $3.5 million loan, and the seller would make mortgage payments on the $2 million loan and keep the balance as payment on his $1.5 million he or she financed.

This is another example of creative financing. Some downside is the risk to both parties, but especially to the buyer. If the buyer pays the holder of the first mortgage (the seller) and the seller doesn't make the payment to the lender, the lender will foreclose.

■ Other Ways to Finance

Sale-Leaseback

A sale-leaseback is an arrangement whereby owners sell their property and then lease it back from the buyer. It's a way to free up cash.

For example, say manufacturers own their building with little or no debt. The manufacturers want to expand their facility and upgrade their equipment but are short of ready cash. The manufacturers could refinance the building, but another alternative is to find a willing buyer. The manufacturers can sell the building to the buyer and agree to lease it back for a period of time. The buyer gets an investment and the manufacturers get ready cash needed. The quality of this investment depends on the viability and credit of the manufacturers.

Conduits

Conduits are an important part of what happens to the loan after it is made. In residential real estate, mortgage money is made available by the lenders selling the loans to investors. As discussed earlier in the chapter, it is more difficult to package and sell commercial loans in the investment (or secondary) market because they tend to be unalike.

Several years ago, some of the large financial institutions packaged some of their commercial loans and sold them to investors. A common name for this is **commercial mortgage backed securities (CMBS)**. The practice became part of the commercial landscape and it has gained and lost popularity as the money markets changed. Those financial groups who package commercial loans are referred to as conduits. Sometimes a conduit loan will offer more aggressive terms than a traditional lender might, or the lender will offer a loan that is not available elsewhere. A downside to a conduit loan is the lack of flexibility in terms and subsequent renegotiation. However, if the terms offered fit the borrower's needs and there is little chance that the borrower will want to come in to renegotiate the loan at a later date, then a conduit loan may be the perfect vehicle for a borrower.

In today's markets, a problem many are facing is how to refinance these CMBS loans. They have a specific due date and unlike a neighborhood bank, the borrower cannot just walk down the street for a meeting with the lender and request a new loan or even an extension. Add to this the fact that many CMBS loans were made as the market was rising and credit terms were much more aggressive. There is over a trillion dollars of CMBS money which will come due over the next three years. Many of the properties financed with CMBS loans have suffered a decline in value and may even be upside down, making it a real challenge to find new financing.

Distressed Properties

Commercial real estate properties experienced great success and demand between 2001 and 2007. Then, as capital sources diminished dramatically, these properties experienced a substantial decrease in demand and value.

A broker is frequently the person owners may turn to when the owners find themselves facing payments they cannot make, or they have a loan coming due which cannot be extended or refinanced. A broker must be aware of the availability of capital, both public and private, to be able to help distressed owners of commercial real estate.

When listing distressed commercial estate, the broker must ask the owner many questions to ascertain the status of transferability. Some of the questions would include, how much debt is owned; when it comes due, who holds the debt; has there been any default; is the property shown as collateral for any other loan; et cetera. The broker also needs to take care to not offer advice beyond the broker's expertise or to inadvertently get into the unauthorized practice of law (UPL) by giving legal advice.

The broker's job is to be the broker. That includes giving the owner a reasonable estimate of likely selling price and closing costs, time on the market, availability of capital and overall market conditions which would affect the sale.

A seller who must bring cash to closing may not be in the position to do so; therefore, some type of workout with the lender (commonly referred to as a short sale) may need to take place or it may be that the property will just go into foreclosure. In any case, the broker needs to be aware of whether or not the seller can complete a transaction with the buyer or if the lender's approval will also be needed. Most states regard the need for lender's approval to be a material fact which must be disclosed to the buyer. Check with your state to know the requirements.

Another area where brokers are finding business is working with the note holders (usually the lender) to find buyers for properties now owned by the note holder or soon to be foreclosed on. It is important for the broker to know the requirements of their note holder clients to properly do the job necessary. As part of the listing, the broker may be asked to do some property management tasks such as routine property inspections, minor maintenance, or rent collection. Again, the broker must insure that he has the proper agreement in place and must be careful to document all activities.

Seller Financing

Often overlooked, seller financing is another source of funds. The seller may prefer to receive monies over a period of time (installment sale) or enjoy the income from the interest on the loan made. A wraparound loan (discussed earlier) may employ seller financing.

There are many things to consider with seller financing, especially for the seller. What protections are there in the case of default? What if the tenant changes? Can the property be damaged and therefore not provide proper security? The buyer needs to consider what protections they have in case of default. An experienced real estate attorney should assist in the preparation of documents and terms. The seller can offer many of the different types of loans described earlier.

Syndications

Syndication refers to the raising of funds through offering an investment opportunity to individuals or lenders. When lenders syndicate a loan, they share the risk and reward with other lenders by dividing the loan up. Some syndicate loans are regulated by state or federal laws. Check with an experienced CPA or attorney.

When a developer syndicates a real estate development, that developer is typically raising equity cash from investors in return for a part of the ownership. While a syndicated property can be 100% financed through investors' contributions, usually the developer has a long-term mortgage loan and raises the equity through the investors.

Syndications may be informal: A developer may seek money from a small group of friends or associates. Or syndications may be quite formal and be considered a security. It is important for a real estate broker to know if what they are selling is a security, as they may need a securities license to sell securities legally. The shares may be sold using a prospectus that outlines the terms of the investment, the risks, and the estimated rewards.

Limited partnerships are a form of syndication. The developer (or their securities agent) sells shares of a property to raise equity. The investors who purchase these shares are limited as to their liability and risk. They are also limited as far as management input goes. They must leave the day-to-day operations to others; otherwise, they may be considered something other than limited partners and have increased liability.

Limited liability companies (LLCs) have replaced many of the limited partnerships as they do much the same thing but help limit liability for the developers. Some LLCs have replaced general partnerships, where all partners are personally liable for the project and its debts.

When deciding on the best ownership structure, a developer should contact their accountant, attorney, or tax advisor. Further, a broker should never give legal or tax advice to a customer or client unless the advice is, "Call a professional!"

■ The Mortgage Instrument

The lender will want some kind of collateral for the loan, so in case the borrower defaults (doesn't pay), the lender can have a means to acquire assets or funds to repay the debt.

For real estate, a lender will use either a **mortgage** or a **deed of trust**. Both have a similar effect—the property is encumbered until the debt is repaid. A mortgage acts as a lien. The borrower retains full title, but the lender has a lien until the mortgage is paid off.

A deed of trust actually conveys legal title to the lender with the borrower retaining equitable title. Once the borrower repays the loan, legal title is granted to the borrower. These mortgage instruments are recorded in the public records.

■ The Loan Process

While it can vary depending on the lender, borrower, and type of loan, the loan process usually goes through the following steps:

Step 1. Borrower makes inquiries to lenders (or mortgage brokers) about availability and terms.

Step 2. Borrower and lender (or mortgage broker) negotiate terms.

Step 3. Once terms are agreed to, a loan commitment letter is issued. The buyer makes application and pays the negotiated fees to the lender

Step 4. Loan closing date is set.

Step 5. During the period between commitment letter and loan closing, the buyer provides necessary documents to the lender. These vary according to the project. For example, let's say we are financing a shopping center that we are purchasing. Some of the documents a borrower might need to supply include the following:

- Tenant leases
- Copies of all contracts for services on the property
- Survey
- Appraisal
- Borrower's financial statement
- Inspection reports

- Title insurance policy, title exam, abstract of title
- Tenant estoppel letters
- Mortgage or deed of trust
- Promissory note
- Borrow affidavit
- Assignment of rents agreement
- Guaranties

Step 6. Some of the above might be finalized at closing, but the borrower usually reviews the draft copy prior to closing. Further negotiations may take place depending on what is discovered during the time between loan commitment and closing.

Step 7. Loan is closed and funds are disbursed. Final fees are paid, and mortgage broker is paid. Documents are recorded. All is well.

Underwriting

The underwriter is the lender's analyst who analyzes the loan offered, the property itself, and the borrower, and then makes a recommendation to the lender about the desirability of the loan.

A couple of important and easy-to-understand issues in **underwriting** involve risk measurement. The best way to illustrate is to look at a sample loan and see how an underwriter might view it.

Let's look at an example.

Underwriting Example

Say that an owner wants to buy a shopping center. The sales price is $20,000,000. He has other centers and has a reputation as an experienced and solid operator. His financials look good.

The borrower would prefer to have an exculpated loan, in other words one that would not require any personal guarantees. Only the real estate (shopping center) would stand as security for the debt. Remember that this is also referred to as a nonrecourse loan (a loan that requires personal guarantees is called a recourse loan).

The lender now looks at the financials of the shopping center.

Income:

Income on grocery (35,000 sq. ft.)	$455,000
+ Income of shops (60,000)	1,200,000
– Less vacancy 10% shops	–120,000
+ Outparcel ground rent	200,000
Total Income	$1,735,000

Operating expenses:

Common area maintenance	$47,000
Real estate taxes	62,000
Insurance	62,000
Management fee	70,000
Administrative	15,000
– Less amount reimbursed	– 225,000
Total Net Expenses	31,000

Net Operating Income (NOI):

Total Income	1,735,000
Less: Total Net Expenses	– 31,000
Equals Net Operating Income	$1,704,000

This net operating income (NOI) is what the owner has left to pay the mortgage, capital expenses, and any income taxes on the property. It may also be referred to as a free and clear return.

There are some factors not shown here. For example, there will be expenses that will need to be amortized (spread out) over some period per Internal Revenue Service (IRS) requirements. Some examples include the following:

■ Brokerage fees

■ Tenant upfitting (cost of finishing out tenant space)

■ Signage

■ Replacement reserves (money set aside to replace capital items such as roof and parking lots, signs)

Although these costs most likely cannot be expensed in the year spent, we all know that these costs will occur and that someone has to pay them.

The lender wants to ensure that there is enough money left each month to pay the mortgage payment. If the lender just looked at the income and expenses, then what about the years when other monies needed to be spent? Could the borrower have enough to cover those?

Let's say that an average yearly allocation of those items listed above is $75,000. Depending on the lending market, an underwriter might subtract $75,000 from the NOI to get an adjusted NOI of $1,629,000. A more aggressive lender may not deduct as much or any.

Let's see the impact of these: We'll start with the original NOI of $1,704,000 from above and look at three scenarios. How much can I borrow?

Assumptions:

■ Loan is 75% LTV (can borrow 75% of the shopping center value).

■ Interest rate is 6%.

■ Schedule is 25 years; term is 15 years (this is not uncommon in commercial real estate and means that a balloon payment will be due at the end of 15 years).

■ Capitalization rate is 9% (cap rate is the rate of return other investors are getting on similar investments; see Chapter 6).

Step 1. Calculate value using the cap rate.

> This assumes that the underwriter agrees with all the numbers presented. What if the market showed a vacancy rate of 20%, not 10%? If you increase vacancy to 20%, that lowers the NOI by about $120,000.
>
> NOI ÷ Cap rate = Value

Step 2. Multiply value by the percentage the lender is willing to loan.

> Value × Percentage = Maximum loan offered

Scenario #1

$1,704,000 ÷ 9% = $18,933,333. Let's round to $19,000,000.

The value is $19,000,000 × 75% loan = $14,250,000 = loan

Scenario #2

What if the NOI was the lower number, $1,629,000, because the lender had subtracted $75,000 in replacement reserves?

$1,629,000 ÷ 9% = $18,100,000 value × 75% loan = $13,575,000 = loan

Scenario #3

What if the vacancy number was 20%, not 10%? The NOI would be $120,000 less.

$1,509,000 ÷ 9% = $16,766,666 × 75% loan = 12,575,000 loan

The difference between the first scenario and the last one is $1,675,000 in loan proceeds, meaning that the owner would need to come up with that much more in addition to the other equity needed.

If the purchase price was $20,000,000 and the loan was $12,575,000, the buyer would need $7,425,000 from his or her own pocket or from another source! The lender also wants to ensure that there is enough to cover the mortgage payment (commonly referred to as "debt service"). This coverage is called **debt service coverage ratio (DSCR)**. It reflects how much above the mortgage payment the lender needs the NOI to be. How much does the NOI need to be to cover the debt service?

If the coverage ratio was 1.20 (spoken as "a one-two-oh coverage ratio"), then the mortgage payment couldn't exceed $1,257,500 on a NOI of $1,509,000 ($1,509,000 ÷ 1.20 = $1,257,500). Using a debt service of $1,257,500, interest of 6%, and payments scheduled over 25 years, the loan could be as much as $16,000,000. But the loan cannot exceed 75% of the value which computed to $12,575,000. Why the big difference?

With a capitalization rate of 9% and a low interest rate of 6%, the DSCR will seldom be an issue. But what if interest rates were to rise to 12%? With the same debt service of $1,257,500, a 12% interest rate, and payments over 25 years, $9,949,600 would be the maximum loan. When interest rates are high or values are low, the DSCR will play a more important role.

The lender uses both loan to value (LTV) ratio and DSCR. Typically the lender will offer to lend only the lower of the two amounts.

We discussed capitalization rates and pro formas in Chapter 6. Remember the lender's primary concern is having the loan repaid, not having to foreclose. If a lender is too conservative, then they may not make any loans. Lending is a delicate balancing act.

■ Summary

If you can finance it, you can sell it. If you cannot finance it, you may still be able to sell it, but your buyer pool will be limited and whatever makes it hard to finance may also affect the value.

By understanding the basics of real estate loan underwriting, a broker can anticipate questions and challenges from the appraiser and lender. A good broker will stay in contact with commercial appraisers and commercial lenders. By doing so, the broker can stay on top of industry trends and have valuable resources when needed.

---

case study   **Underwriter**

Now you be the underwriter. Developer Lamar is buying an office building in a growing market. It is fairly full and well located. He has been a good customer. List five things you want to know before approving the loan.

Length of tenant leases.

Rates of leasing

Fixed expenses

Cap Rate of purchase.

Loan amount.

■ Review Questions

1. When seeking a loan from a large life insurance company, the probable contact would be a
   a. life insurance company.
   b. mortgage broker.
   c. real estate broker.
   d. local bank executive.

2. The *BEST* place to get a short-term bridge or acquisition loan would be a
   a. local bank.
   b. life insurance company.
   c. real estate investment trust.
   d. pension fund.

3. On a very large commercial project, which lender would be the *LEAST* likely to make the loan?
   a. Local bank
   b. Life insurance company
   c. REIT
   d. Pension fund

4. A loan that includes another existing loan is referred to as
   a. a conduit loan.
   b. an acquisition loan.
   c. a bridge loan.
   d. a wraparound loan.

5. What is the lender's primary goal?
   a. To make a 10% return
   b. To be repaid
   c. To foreclose
   d. All of these

part 3

Careers in Commercial Real Estate

chapter eight

Brokerage Fundamentals

overview

Now that you have a strong foundation in the ins and outs of commercial real estate, it's time to think about where you see yourself fitting in. We will start by looking at the broker's role, how to start your business as a broker, and what others look for in their broker. ■

learning objectives

When you have completed this chapter, you will be able to

- explain the duties of a broker,
- describe the different types of representation agreements,
- list the common terms in a listing agreement, and
- cite who you represent in a transaction.

■ Key Terms

agency agreement

broker

client

co-brokerage agreement (co-broke agreement)

commercial information exchange (CIE)

customer

dual agency

employment agreement

exclusive agency agreement

exclusive buyer agency agreement

exclusive right to lease agreement

exclusive right to sell agreement

exclusive tenant representation agreement

nonexclusive buyer agency agreement

nonexclusive right to lease agreement

nonexclusive tenant representation agreement

open listing

protection agreement

protection period

registration of prospects

tenant representative (tenant rep)

transactional brokerage

To keep things simple and to get you comfortable with the language of commercial real estate, we will use the term **broker** to mean any type of real estate licensee. Most states have two types of real estate licensees—salesperson and broker. A salesperson must be supervised by a broker or work under a broker. While some commercial agents hold a salesperson license, they may refer to themselves as brokers, not meaning to misrepresent, but using the term to imply that they are "brokering" a transaction. A few states have only broker licensees. This won't make a difference for our purposes.

■ How Commercial Brokerage Works

When should an owner or buyer use a commercial real estate broker? As a broker, I think that unless buyers or sellers are in the business or know the market well, they should seek the advice of a qualified broker. While most brokers offer an array of services, most will be willing to contract for only those services needed by a buyer or seller. Not all brokers may offer the same services. In fact, in commercial real estate, brokers may specialize and offer unique services for a market niche or a particular industry. The following are types of services a broker may offer:

- Market property for sale or lease, including advertising, calling likely prospects or other brokers who represent potential buyers, and posting the property in a listing service such as a **commercial information exchange (CIE)**
- Recommend a listing price by using market comparables
- Negotiate a contract or lease agreement
- Recommend other professionals, such as mortgage bankers and brokers, architects, engineers, land-use specialists, attorneys, contractors, appraisers
- Share knowledge about local laws and ordinances, such as zoning and building codes
- Provide information about the local economy, industries, and economics
- Find suitable property for sale, particularly unlisted property
- Recommend an offering price and terms
- Locate suitable tenants for space
- Locate suitable space for tenants
- Identify property for investors based on investor's criteria
- Identify investors to invest in a client's property
- Assist in the performance of some of the due diligence inspection items

Perhaps a seller has a property for sale and many potential buyers have called about it. The seller is happy to see so many potential buyers, but which one should he or she choose? The seller may hire a broker solely for advice about which offer to accept or pursue. Further, the seller may need the broker to assist in the contract negotiation. The broker must be careful to not step over the line to be guilty of practicing law. One must have a law license to give legal advice. The broker may use personal expertise about the market to recommend what to offer and what terms are reasonable.

A tenant may wish to hire a **tenant representative (tenant rep)**, a specific type of broker, to help them find space in an unfamiliar market. Unless the tenant's company has a real estate department that can perform this service, the tenant does not know what the market is like or the terms being offered. A local broker who is active in the market will be able to advise the tenant. Once the space is located, the tenant may or may not turn over all negotiation to their legal department and tell the broker that their work together is done.

Still, a new buyer may want a broker to help him in every step of the transaction: locate the property; suggest an offering price; help negotiate the contract; recommend an attorney, builder, lender, et cetera; coordinate the due diligence inspections; work with the seller and the seller's attorney; attend the closing; and assist after the closing in the development or leasing of the property.

A broker's job is as varied as the types of markets and buyers in commercial real estate.

Real Estate Careers

Where can one go with a real estate license? Just about anywhere with the proper knowledge and training. Depending on the market, a real estate professional may be a specialist or may be more of a generalist, doing a little of everything. Remember to check your state's license laws regarding licensed activity. Also, if you plan to work outside of your state, make sure you are properly licensed in the state(s) where you work. License laws are different in each state.

Let's look at some avenues you may wish to investigate:

General brokerage. The general broker represents buyers and sellers as well as landlords and tenants on a variety of property types. Depending on the market, the broker may handle several property types. The broker may also develop some property and manage his or her own properties and some properties for others.

Landlord representative. The broker represents a landlord's property or properties.

Tenant representative. The broker represents the tenants' interests. A broker may work for one tenant, but unless that tenant is seeking many spaces, a broker would need to represent several tenants to earn a reasonable income.

Specialist. Brokers in larger markets need to specialize because there is just too much product to be knowledgeable in all types. A broker may specialize in retail (mall, power centers, neighborhood centers, freestanding retail, restaurants, etc.), office (central business, suburban, highrise, medical, etc.), industrial (multitenant, single tenant, research, warehouse, manufacturing, office/showroom, etc.), land (to be developed as housing subdivisions, shopping centers, office buildings, etc.), or institutional (churches, government, schools, etc.). A broker may also work for an end user, such as a retailer, and be that retainer's point person for real estate selections.

Property management. A property manager manages real estate for others. This person may also specialize in a particular type of real estate (office, retail, industrial, freestanding, malls, mixed use, etc.). Property management is covered in greater detail in Chapter 11.

Development. A broker may work alone or with others to create buildings. Depending on the market, a developer may specialize in a particular product type, such as neighborhood shopping centers anchored by a particular grocery store. There are many aspects to development careers, including leasing of tenant space, acquiring the land, working with the contractors and architects, negotiating the financing, or working with the tenants. The development process is quite lengthy and is covered in detail in Chapter 10.

Consulting.   Once you have experience in an area, you can hire yourself out to help others in commercial real estate. Perhaps you are a restaurant expert, a feasibility specialist, a finance guru, a crisis manager. Many people are looking for a consulting broker to help them in one area or another.

Financing.   While not actually a real estate track, someone who understands income-producing real estate and financing can find a career in mortgage brokerage or mortgage banking.

Syndication.   Selling shares of real estate properties to investors falls into the category of syndication. This sales area may require a securities license as well.

This list can go on because there are no rules limiting what you can do with your real estate knowledge and skills. If one career path doesn't suit you, try another. The areas can be so very different, but you can bring what you've learned from each one to make you more competent and successful.

My own career has been varied and extremely fulfilling. In more than 30 years in the business, I've been fortunate to try many things; I learned much from each one; and I think the following experiences have added to my competence:

- Apartment leasing agent
- Apartment manager
- Apartment specialist—opened new properties and closed out those sold
- Apartment development—worked with lenders, investors, architects, etc., to build new apartment complexes and open them
- Administrative—worked for a national real estate developer and manager in a regional office handling special projects and human resource issues
- Property manager for commercial properties—managed retail, office, and industrial properties in several states
- Commercial development—worked with developers handling various aspects of the commercial development process such as financing, design, leasing, and construction
- Renovation and redevelopment of existing properties
- Refinancing of a large portfolio of properties
- Development and leasing of medical office
- Syndication of medical office
- Consulting—my primary practice now, volunteer activities permitting
- Real estate education and training
- Course writing
- Activity in real estate organizations
- Service on the Planning Commission and Zoning Board of Adjustment
- Service in local, state, and national REALTOR® associations

Agency Agreements

An **agency agreement** is an employment contract between a buyer, seller, landlord, or tenant and a real estate firm. Typically the agency agreement belongs to the firm or broker-in-charge. A broker is assigned to the transaction—the broker who brought the deal in. Acting as an agent may have legal ramifications to both the agent and the principal (buyer, seller, landlord, or tenant). State laws and regulations will control this, but typically an agent owes certain duties to his or her principal. These duties may or may not be spelled out; they may be implied either by common law or by case law or are stated in state statutes, regulations, or administrative rules.

If I am acting as your agent and I make a mistake or misrepresent you, you, as my principal, may also be held liable. If I make a promise without your approval, you may be required to honor my promise even if you don't agree. In the eyes of the law of most states, an agent stands in place of his or her principal. Generally, as your agent, I owe you certain duties—loyalty, honesty, obedience, accurate accounting of money and documents, disclosure of all facts that might affect your decision, confidentially, skill, care, and diligence.

Individual states govern the conduct of their licensees, and each state has its own set of regulations. Check with the real estate commission in your state for a copy of any regulations that apply to agency agreements, agency relationships, and nonagency relationships. We'll look at important agency agreement clauses later on in this chapter. Let's look at typical agency agreements.

Exclusive right to sell. The **exclusive right to sell agreement** is between seller and agent (firm) and gives the firm the exclusive right to handle the sale of the property. In the event that the seller finds a buyer, the firm still receives the commission on the sale. A seller can list his or her property with only one firm. As with any agreement, it can be modified. For example, let's say a seller wants to list his property for sale but has been negotiating with his neighbor to sell it to him. When the seller lists his property with a broker, he may not want to owe a commission if the neighbor buys it, so the seller would exclude the sale to the neighbor but agree to pay the broker a commission if it's sold to anyone else during the listing period.

Exclusive agency. The **exclusive agency agreement** is similar to the exclusive right to sell agreement except that any sale done by the owner is excluded. In other words, the seller reserves the right to sell it himself or herself and not owe a commission. He or she can list with only one real estate firm.

Open listing. With an **open listing**, the seller can give the listing to as many real estate firms as he or she wants. The firm that secures a buyer is the one that gets the commission. If the seller sells the property herself or himself, then she or he doesn't owe a commission.

Exclusive buyer agency. In an **exclusive buyer agency agreement** (also called an exclusive buyer representation agreement) the buyer agrees to use only one firm to represent him or her in finding property to buy. The buyer agrees to direct all inquiries to the firm and if the buyer locates property on their own, the buyer will notify the broker so the broker can be involved. We will discuss compensation when we review the terms of these agreements.

Nonexclusive buyer agency. With a **nonexclusive buyer agency agreement**, the buyer can hire as many firms as desired. The one who finds the property that the buyer buys receives the commission.

Exclusive tenant representation. In an **exclusive tenant representation agreement**, the tenant agrees to use only one firm to represent him or her to find space and negotiate a lease.

Nonexclusive tenant representation.   The **nonexclusive tenant represen-tation agreement** allows the tenant to use as many firms as desired. The firm that secures the space desired by the tenant is due the commission and represents the tenant in the transaction.

Exclusive right to lease.   With the **exclusive right to lease agreement**, the landlord gives one firm the right to find tenants for the property. Commission is paid according to the agreement.

Nonexclusive right to lease.   The landlord can use as many firms as desired to lease the property in a **nonexclusive right to lease agreement**. The firm that brings a tenant who leases the property earns the commission.

Dual agency.   Some states do not allow **dual agency**. In those states where dual agency is allowed and practiced, the firm now represents both sides of the trans-action—both the landlord and tenant or both the buyer and seller. There may be different brokers working with each, but all brokers work for the same firm. Dual agency must be agreed to by all of the parties in advance. Duties must be clearly explained and spelled out in the agreement.

Transactional brokerage, facilitation, or intermediation.   While not a traditional agency agreement, **transactional brokerage**—also known as facilita-tion or intermediation—replaces some agency agreements in states where it is practiced. The firm is employed to perform certain duties for a buyer or seller or landlord or tenant. No agency relationship is created or implied. Check with your state to see if transactional brokerage is allowed there.

Other Agreements

Some other agreements commonly used in the brokerage business are described below.

Co-brokerage.   The **co-brokerage agreement (co-broke agreement)** is used to set up commission splits between firms. Let's say I'm the listing agent on a piece of land. You represent a buyer. You call me to learn more about the land, then ask me, "What's the commission?" I tell you what I'll pay your firm if your buyer buys. The co-broke agreement is signed by both of us confirming our agreement.

Protection.   The **protection agreement** is used to confirm commission paid to a broker's firm by an unrepresented owner. Let's say I represent a buyer looking for land. I ask John, a landowner of unlisted land, if he'd be willing to sell. John says he is. In addition to getting all the information from him, I ask him how much commission he will pay me if my buyer buys. Keep in mind that I'm not the seller's agent; I am the buyer's agent. However, the seller can pay me, and, if he agrees to do so, I need to have that agreement in writing.

Employment.   An **employment agreement** is between the firm and the broker. It sets up commission splits between the firm and the broker and outlines any duties, agreements and promises of each. This is very important for every agent and firm to have as it helps avoid misunderstandings of payments and specifies what happens when a broker leaves a firm.

Agreement Terms

Let's look at the following key points that a listing agreement needs to address:

- Names of the firm and client(s)
- Term of agreement (start and termination)

- Whether the agreement is exclusive or not
- Client's permission to cooperate with other firms
- Client's permission to offer subagency, dual agency
- Property description
- Listing terms (price, seller financing, possession, other terms, lease terms offered)
- Client's permission to advertise
- The party who pays marketing expenses
- Client's agreement to cooperate with firm by referring queries to firm
- Payment of commission (entitlement, calculation, method and timing of payment), payment of commission on options or leases, extensions.
- **Protection period**—a broker requirement that if a prospect the broker introduced to the client during the agency period buys or leases within a certain time period after the agreement has expired, then the firm is still entitled to the commission—included in order to discourage a client from delaying a transaction to avoid paying a commission
- **Registration of prospects**—stipulating that the client must provide a list of any prospects who have seen the property and the brokers involved
- Variety of contractual items (authority to contract, bankruptcy, indemnification, parties, entire agreement, governing law, etc.)
- Signature blocks—important that whomever signs on behalf of the client has the authority to do so or the broker may end up working for free
- Any terms, disclosures, or notices required by state regulation

Now, the following looks at what a buyer representation agreement needs to address (also applies to tenant representation):

- Names of the firm and client(s)
- Term of agreement (start and termination)
- Whether it is exclusive or not
- Territory covered
- Client's permission to cooperate with other firms
- Client's permission to offer subagency, dual agency
- Terms desired (price, seller financing, possession, other terms, lease terms offered)
- Client's agreement to cooperate with firm by referring queries to firm
- Payment of commission (who pays, entitlement, calculation, method and timing of payment), payment of commission on options or leases, extensions, etc.
- Protection period—broker requirement that if a property the broker introduced to the client during the agency period is bought or leased by the client within a certain time period after the agreement has expired, then the firm is still entitled to the commission—included in order to discourage a client from delaying a transaction to avoid paying a commission
- Registration of properties—requirement that the client provide a list of any properties they have seen and the brokers involved
- Variety of contractual items (authority to contract, bankruptcy, indemnification, parties, entire agreement, governing law, etc.)

- Signature blocks—important that whomever signs on behalf of the client has the authority to do so
- Any terms, disclosures, or notices required by state regulation

Developing Relationships with Clients and Customers

Before we move on, let's clarify our terms: A **client** is one with whom a firm has an agency relationship; a **customer** is one with whom the firm may be working but with whom the firm does not have an agency relationship.

For example, Sue is the leasing agent for an office building. She represents the owner of the building, Jonathon Finch, and her firm has an exclusive-right-to-lease contract with him. She receives a call from ABD Widgets. They are looking for space such as Sue has listed. She correctly asks if they have a broker. They reply, "No"; they will represent themselves. Jonathon is the client, and ABD Widgets is a customer, even though Sue is helping them.

Sue must be honest with ABD Widgets but owes them no advocacy or advice. She must work in the best interest of her client, the building owner, Jonathon. If she knows of a better deal ABD Widgets can make, she needs to keep it to herself because she is not their agent.

Let's try a more complicated example. Let's say that Ned Demidov, who also works for Sue's firm, represents ABD Widgets. After careful study of their needs, Ned realizes that Jonathon's building (his firm's listing) is the best location for them. In most states, the firm must now act as a dual agent, representing both sides but favoring neither party over the other. To practice dual agency in their state, Ned and Sue must get written permission from their clients to proceed. They must explain what they can and cannot do as dual agents. Check your state laws to see the requirements and options concerning dual agency, if it is allowed there at all.

Where can a broker find clients or even customers? Some detailed suggestions are provided in Chapter 1. Another method is to target certain industries and get to know the needs and wants of that business.

For example, an office broker may specialize in medical office space, which is very different than typical office space. After the broker has learned about the office needs of doctors, the broker can assist by knowing which office buildings in the market are suitable for doctors' offices and sell that service to the medical community by calling on existing doctors' offices and hospital administrators. Once the broker gains a reputation for knowing the needs of the medical community, then word gets around and referrals will begin. The relationships are being created.

Another way to create relationships is to work with a user who will need multiple locations. Remember that to be effective, you must have local market knowledge or work with a broker who does. Knowing the user's needs saves the client time in breaking in a new broker, and once the client's needs are filled, the broker may be able to use that industry knowledge with other users.

The best agency agreement cannot replace trust and confidence. Good brokers are always looking after the best interests of their clients. The agreement is important because it confirms expectations on both sides.

Selling Versus Leasing

Sometimes a client looking for space to lease will realize that buying is a better choice and vice versa. A knowledgeable broker will know how to qualify a client to see what the best avenue is. Sometimes it can be either. A sharp broker will have both situations covered in the agency agreement, even if the client is insistent on leasing only.

A very good friend of mine had just entered the commercial brokerage business when he landed a listing on an office building. He negotiated an attractive rate of commission and promptly found a potential buyer. The buyer offered the seller a lease purchase contract—the buyer would lease the building for up to 10 years at a set rental rate and could buy the building at any time at a set price. The seller quickly agreed.

My friend called me to ask how much commission he should get. I referred him to his agency agreement with the seller (in North Carolina, one must have a written agency agreement before one can perform any brokerage duties for another). He said that the agreement stated commission for a sale but not for a lease. I suggested that his commission might be 0%. He didn't much like that and negotiated a fair amount with the owner. He was lucky. Some owners might not be so fair. He told me that in the future he would not leave his commission to chance. He'd make sure anything he could think of would be addressed in the agency agreement. This is a good plan for any broker.

A broker should always do an analysis of selling versus leasing. An example of this analysis is shown in Chapter 6. Local market conditions may make one a better choice than the other.

■ What Clients Look For When Hiring a Broker

To sell your services, you have to know what people need—plus their wants and desires. What do clients look for in a broker? They look for the same things I would look for, which include the following:

- Experience in the type of property desired (I don't want to be a training ground, usually. Sometimes, it may pay to groom a broker for your account. As a new broker, if you can hook up with a seasoned investor who is willing to groom and train you, that's a great opportunity!)

- Experience and knowledge of the area or location (Many times it's not what you know but who you know. This is especially true for commercial real estate brokerage. I want a broker who is connected, and who might be able to find things other brokers wouldn't know about. This is why community involvement is so important.)

- Who else the broker is representing (I don't want to be the lowest priority or one of many wanting the same services or property type. As a broker, you want quality not quantity when it comes to clients.)

- How busy the broker is (If the broker is overbooked, then I may not get the attention I want or need. If the broker has nothing to do, why?)

- References from those I trust

- Work style compatible with mine

- Responsiveness

- Follows up well

- Does not reveal vital details of transactions to others
- Offers a fair agency agreement with fair compensation and terms
- Has a good reputation in the field (I may be judged by the broker I hire.)
- Speaks frankly (Bad news given as freely as the good. I need to know everything to make my best decision.)
- Has few or no conflicts of interest (I need unqualified loyalty.)
- Technologically savvy, or has an assistant who is

Overall I need a broker I can trust, who works well with me, and who understands my needs and wants to get the job done. I may work with several brokers at once, all with different areas of expertise. As a client, I owe them my loyalty and trust, and I need to be honest, reasonable, and responsive to their requests.

While commercial real estate brokerage is different than residential brokerage, there still is a people factor involved. Buyers and tenants find someone competent they like, trust, and can work with.

■ Summary

Understanding the nature of the business and what clients look for in a broker can help you organize your business plan. From time to time, reread your business plan, make adjustments, and plan for your future.

| case study | **Agency Agreements** |

You call on a landowner and want to list his property. He already has some folks who have shown interest and states that he will not pay you if any of them buy. He is not ready to actively list, does not want a "For Sale" sign, is not in any rush to sell, but says he'll be happy to pay you if you bring a buyer and they agree on terms. Which agency agreements would most likely suit his needs and protect you?

_____

_____

_____

_____

_____

■ Review Questions

1. How is a commercial information exchange (CIE) different from a multiple listing service (MLS)?

   a. There is no difference.

   b. No blanket offer of compensation or cooperation exists.

   c. The MLS is for residential property only; the CIE is for commercial property only.

   d. The commission is stated in the CIE but not in the MLS.

2. Which document should be used to arrange for any sharing of commission between the listing broker and the selling broker?

   a. Exclusive right to sell agreement

   b. One time showing agreement

   c. Protection agreement

   d. Co-brokerage agreement

3. As a listing agent, which agreement affords you the *MOST* protection and control of the transaction and seller?

   a. Exclusive right to sell agreement

   b. Exclusive agency agreement

   c. Protection agreement

   d. Dual agency agreement

4. Which duty shown below would an agent be *LEAST* likely to do for a buyer client under an agency agreement?

   a. Find suitable property

   b. Assist in locating lenders

   c. Assist with due diligence items

   d. Give legal and tax advice

5. What are the *MOST* important traits buyers will seek in their real estate broker?

   a. A strong balance sheet

   b. Experience, trust, and loyalty

   c. An exciting car

   d. Membership in the client's country club

chapter nine

Leasing

overview

Many brokers start in commercial real estate leasing. It can be easier to start one's career working with a known product (a developer's) than trying to get listings or represent buyers. By concentrating on one owner's property or properties, a new broker can gain expertise and credibility. While leasing may seem simple to do, the lease terms and the leasing process can be quite complex. Good brokers will advise their tenants or landlord owners of the current market and impact of certain lease terms. We'll cover the leasing process, key lease terms, using a broker, and being the broker. ■

learning objectives

When you have completed this chapter, you will be able to

■ describe the leasing process including timelines, and

■ define lease terms and different types of leases.

■ Key Terms

breakpoint	ground lease	rentable
expense stop	net lease	triple net lease
expense cap	pass-through expense	upfitting
full service lease	percentage rent clause	usable
gross lease		

■ Leasing Commercial Space

Leasing is not as easy to do as many people think. A tenant is asking to use someone else's property for a period of time. The parties (landlord and tenant) must agree to all kinds of terms (found in the lease) so that everyone knows their rights, responsibilities, and duties. When someone, an individual investor or a company, buys a building, they can do most anything they want within the law and subject to existing leases. This is not so when leasing space. A tenant may be subject to not only laws and regulations but to agreements made with other tenants (use clause), requirements in the loan documents, and whatever restrictions the landlord has in the lease.

With businesses changing, it's tough for a tenant to agree to be constrained to the type of business they may have in their space. What seems like a long-term business venture today may be gone tomorrow due to new regulations, market conditions, competition, tax laws, zoning changes, cultural shifts, and so on. A good example seen in early 2000 was the rise and fall of many dot-coms. For a while, the dot-coms were taking space faster than it could be built. Then the dot-coms disappeared, leaving expensive vacant space behind. Now, in 2013, we are seeing them making a softer comeback. This had another effect: Not only was a source of space users shrinking, but the space they left behind flooded some markets with excess space, driving the rental rates down. When companies tried to lighten their losses by subleasing or assigning their unneeded space to others, some chose to do so at bargain rates, causing market uncertainty. Landlords were nervous because there was downward pressure on rents and existing tenants now had other space choices when their leases expired.

A lease can also take more time to complete than expected. Leasing finished, move-in ready space may not be as much of a challenge as space that needs finishing. The terms commonly used for the need to finish a space to meet a tenant's needs are tenant **upfitting**, also known as tenant improvements or tenant build out. In the lease negotiation, the tenant negotiates upfitting costs as well as rent and other terms. The amount of upfitting can be one of the most important parts of the deal for both the landlord and the tenant. It's not unlike building a new home. The builder who offers more incentives to the buyer may get the contract.

■ The Leasing Process

Let's look at the leasing process. The approximate time to accomplish each step is included, but keep in mind that because these time estimates are based on a sample transaction, the actual times could vary widely.

Step 1. A broker meets with a potential tenant seeking space. The broker interviews the tenant to ascertain needs and wants. Some of the things a broker needs to know are the following:

- Size of space needed
- Configuration of space
- Utilities needed
- Access to the building (hours of operation)
- Proximity to customers and to other businesses, such as suppliers
- Tenant mix
- Environmental issues
- Special equipment used by tenant
- Storage
- Waste disposal
- Security needed
- Rail access needed
- Floor loads

- Ceiling heights
- Zoning needed
- Signage required
- Visibility
- Budget for rent
- Location
- Expansion expectations
- Parking needed
- Approval process and time frame
- Any space previously seen and any brokers used
- Where they are currently located and why they are moving
- Financial strength and credit rating
- Amenities needed in the building and in the area
- Any special requirements
- Access for loading and unloading
- What the tenant currently has for space

The list goes on.

Step 2.   (One week.) After the broker gets some guidelines, the broker must find suitable properties for the tenant to view.

Step 3.   (Two weeks.) The tenant tours all of the likely spaces and narrows the choices down to two.

Step 4.   (One week.) The broker will ask the two properties' representatives to submit proposals based on the tenant's requirements.

Step 5.   (One week.) The tenant and broker will discuss negotiating strategy and develop counteroffers to one or both proposals. While all this can happen quickly, keep in mind that trying to schedule meetings takes more time than anything else.

Step 6.   (One week.) Responses to the counters are returned to the tenant's broker. Another meeting is scheduled, or the proposals can be e-mailed to the tenant and a phone call may suffice as the meeting. This can be done the same day via e-mail or take weeks depending on who needs to make the decision. Let's use a week.

Step 7.   The counteroffer process can take a very long or a very short time to work through. In the end, the tenant selects building A.

Step 8.   (Two weeks.)—Either the tenant or the building representative begins preparation of the actual lease. Again, if this is a straightforward deal, using the building's or tenant's standard lease form, then the lease may be e-mailed to the broker and tenant or landlord in a matter of days. If it's an attorney-drafted lease, then it may take much longer.

Step 9.   (One week to one month.) In practice, many leases need additional negotiations.

Step 10.   (One hour to two weeks.) Once all the terms are agreed to as written and everyone's legal counsel has reviewed it, it's time to execute the agreement.

The tenant may have the authority to sign it on the spot or it may need to be sent to the tenant's home office. The same is true for the landlord. Keep in mind that any party could still back out entirely at this stage.

By the end of this step, the lease is executed. Let's say that according to the listing broker's listing agreement and the co-broke agreement, half of the commission is due to the brokers upon lease execution. The balance is due when the tenant takes possession. Payment of the commission is negotiable between the broker and the building owner. If the agreement states that the listing broker is to share the commission with the tenant's broker, then the co-brokerage agreement needs to specify when and how commission will be shared. Obviously a listing broker wants any payment to the tenant's broker to coincide with their payment from the owner.

Step 11. (Two weeks.) Once the lease is executed, work on the tenant space begins. Rough plans may have been drawn up to get cost estimates, or the entire plan may already be complete, or nothing may have even been started. It often takes around a week to finalize drawings and send for pricing. Also, permits will need to be obtained and contractors lined up, which will take an additional week.

Step 12. (Two weeks to several months.) Construction finally begins. Depending on the size of the space, complexity of upfitting and availability of the contractors, the completion may take weeks or months. Remember, upfitting is the process of building out the tenant's space in accordance to their specifications.

Step 13. Construction is finished! The tenant inspects the space, creates a punch list (a list of items that need further attention), then accepts possession of the space. The lease is now in effect. The lease commencement date could be any date—date of possession, date of substantial completion, a particular calendar date, a certain number of days following execution; whatever is agreed to by the parties. The brokers are happy to see the other part of their commission paid. Keep in mind that the rent commencement date may or may not be the same date, so read the documents!

From this example, you can see that leasing space could be quick—all of the decision makers at the table, space completed and leased "as is," and the landlord's standard form lease used. It could be done in a week or even less! Then again, a more complex transaction could take weeks or months. The average time listed in the steps above gives us an approximate transaction time of 13 to 25 weeks.

■ Commercial Leases

There are a number of commercial lease types—in fact the number could be infinite because leases are typically a combination of types. For simplicity, we will look at the basic lease types below.

Gross Lease

The landlord, in a **gross lease**, pays all expenses, and the tenant's rent is one set amount, which may be subject to increases.

Net Lease

With a **net lease** the tenant pays some or all of the expenses of the property, including but not limited to, utilities, real estate taxes, insurance, common area maintenance, utilities, and repairs.

Some leases are referred to as **triple net leases**. Usually triple net means the following are paid by the tenant: common area maintenance (CAM), real estate taxes, and insurance. Always ask clarification of what is passed through. In a recent class, I asked a group of 75 commercial brokers to define "triple net lease." Since they were all from the same geographic market, I didn't expect much variance in the responses. I was wrong! About half the responses were similar, but the other half were all over the place! The lesson learned? Never assume—always ask!

Pass-through expenses refer to expenses paid by the tenant. This payment can be made in two ways: The entire share of the tenant's portion may be passed through for the tenant to pay, or only a portion over a fixed amount—referred to as an **expense stop**—may be passed through.

For example, the lease states that the tenant will pay expenses over the base year (usually the first full year) amount (be sure to have a good definition of expenses). Let's say the base year expense number is $7 per square foot. The next year's expenses are $7.15 per square foot. The tenant would owe $0.15 times their square footage as additional rent.

To determine a tenant's share, follow the lease definition. It can be so much per square foot as seen above or a percentage of the total expense. To calculate the tenant's share of the total, you generally take the tenant's square footage divided by the leasable area of the building or center.

For example, a tenant has 1,500 square feet. The building has leasable square footage of 45,000 square feet. The tenant's share is 1,500 ÷ 45,000 = 3.3%.

A way a tenant may control expenses is to have an **expense cap**. With an expense cap, the tenant agrees to pay pass-through expenses but only up to a maximum amount set by the cap.

For example, a tenant has 1,500 square feet and pays pass-through expenses but has an expense stop of $2.50 per square foot on common area maintenance (CAM). When CAM is $2.30 per square foot, the tenant pays their share. (1500 × $2.30 = $3,450). In fact, the tenant pays their share until CAM exceeds $2.50 per square foot. Let's say that CAM goes up to $2.65 per square foot in the next year. Instead of paying 1,500 square feet × $2.65 = $3,975, this tenant would pay 1,500 square feet × $2.50 = $3,750, because their obligation to pay is "stopped" at $2.50 per square foot.

Full Service Lease

Typically an office lease where the landlord provides all services, such as janitorial, is a **full service lease**. It is usually a form of a gross lease; although some expenses may be passed through.

Ground Lease

An agreement in which land is being leased is called a **ground lease**. In order for development to occur, a ground lease needs to have a long enough term for the lessee to recoup their investment. Some are as short as 10 years; others can be as long as 99 years! At the end of a ground lease, improvements may revert to the landowner, but it depends on the terms of the lease.

Retail Lease With a Percentage Rent Clause

This type of lease may be a net lease or gross lease. The key is the **percentage rent clause**, whereby the lease states that once a tenant's sales exceed a stated amount, the tenant will pay additional rent. This amount is typically calculated by subtracting the gross sales from the stated amount and multiplying that by the stated percentage.

For example, a tenant's lease requires a tenant to pay percentage rent over its natural **breakpoint** at a rate of 6%. The tenant's annual base rent is $30,000. To compute the natural breakpoint, divide the base rent by the percentage: $30,000 ÷ 6% = $500,000.

The tenant will owe additional rent of 6% of gross sales exceeding $500,000. If sales are $650,000 for the year, the additional rent would be: $650,000 − $500,000 = $150,000 × 6% = $9,000.

A retail broker will explain what is possible in a given market. The breakpoint may be artificially set to whatever the parties agree on.

There are many other hybrid forms of leases. The best advice is to ask who pays what and when. Then carefully read the lease to compare. A net lease may carry a lower rental rate, but when you add in the expenses, the gross lease may cost less. Pass-throughs may vary widely from lease to lease. Compare the expense stops to better calculate the true cost of occupancy.

Also pay attention to upfitting costs paid. Having to pay $150,000 up front to finish a space may be an expense not expected. The rent may not seem such a good deal then.

How to Measure Space

Because financial obligations may be tied to the square footage of the space being leased (rent, CAM, taxes, etc.), it is important to know how the space is measured. As a leasing agent, be sure to remember to ask how space is measured in each contract you see so that you can accurately compare proposals. Don't rely on industry jargon.

Here are some of the most common terms and what they may mean. Again, be sure to always ask which of these terms a lease uses and how they are defined.

Rentable. If the rent per square is quoted "per rentable square foot," that usually means that a portion of the shared space of the building is being allocated to each tenant. This allocation may be referred to as a core factor or a load. The total **rentable** square footage of a building is the gross square footage less any penetrations in the floor (for a multistory building). Penetrations include such things as elevator shafts, stairwells, chases, and flues. Think of rentable space as the space that you can stand on.

Usable. If the rent per square is being quoted "per usable square foot," that usually means that the tenant is paying only for their actual space. **Usable** space does not include common areas used by all tenants, such as lobbies, mechanical areas, hallways, bathrooms shared by all tenants, et cetera. Rentable and usable are typically used for "shared" space, in an office building or in a enclosed shopping center. Always ask how space is measured to that you can quote "apples to apples" when comparing spaces.

Here is an example:

Measuring Space

Let's say the gross floor area in a building is 25,000 square feet. Of that, 24,000 square feet are rentable.

Based on the design of the tenants' spaces, let's say usable space is 21,428 square feet.

The relationship of rentable to usable is R ÷ U = 1.12, which is a 12% load.

If a tenant needs 3,000 square feet of usable space, its rentable space would be 3,000 sq. ft. × 1.12 = 3,360 rentable sq. ft. The tenant is paying a portion of the shared areas.

For Example:

Now, Rick needs 2,500 square feet of space. He likes two buildings. Building A quotes $18 per square foot rentable with a load factor of 15%. Building B quotes $20 per square foot usable. Which is the better deal for Rick?

■ Building A: 2,500 sq. ft. × 115% × $18 = $51,750/yr.

■ Building B: 2,500 sq. ft. × $20 = $50,000/yr.

The rent for Building B is less than Building A. If all other terms are the same, then Building B may be the best choice for Rick.

Lease Clauses

In Chapter 5, we listed important lease clauses to consider. We focused on the business issues and didn't go into all the detail necessary for an informed decision about any particular situation. For that, please acquire the services of an experienced commercial broker and your real estate attorney.

■ Using a Leasing Broker

When does an owner need a broker, and when can the owner go it alone? Owners need to ask themselves some hard questions. As a broker, you need to anticipate these questions and answers in order to show the owners why they need your services.

The following are questions I ask owners to ask themselves:

1. Do I know all of the competition in my market?
2. Do I know any concessions being given?
3. Do I understand the impact of all of the lease clauses?
4. Do I know if the tenant is financially able and solvent?
5. Can I locate suitable tenants?
6. Do I have a competent real estate attorney who can help me?
7. Do I have the time to devote to this?
8. Is this the best use of my time?
9. Are there brokers available who are more competent than I am?

If the answers to 1 through 8 are "yes" and 9 is "no," then the owner may not need a broker. Otherwise, obtaining the services of a broker is likely a good idea.

Following are questions I ask tenants to ask themselves:

1. Do I have someone who understands real estate in my company?
2. Does my legal counsel have experience in lease negotiation?
3. Has my company negotiated other successful leases I can use as a guide?
4. Do I know the market well?
5. Do I know the market rates and terms offered?
6. Is this the best use of my time?
7. Do I have plenty of time to do my research?
8. Do I already know where I want or need to locate?
9. Are there brokers who are more competent than I am?

Again, only if the answers to 1 through 8 are "yes" and 9 is "no," would it be likely that the tenant did not need a broker.

Generally, an owner or a tenant is not in the real estate business. They wouldn't try to install their own phones, so why would they try to handle one of their most important decisions that will affect their business every day?

An experienced broker has seen it all and knows what to ask and can anticipate needs. In addition, an experienced broker should be able to save the owner or tenant money by

- allowing the owners or tenants to remain focused on their business;
- getting the best deal possible for the client; and
- recommending alternatives not considered before.

You've probably noticed that I keep using the adjective *experienced* when referring to a broker, accountant, or attorney. A broker, accountant, or attorney who is not experienced in a particular type of transaction can cause more harm than good. They don't know what they don't know and neither do you.

I cannot overemphasize the need to qualify any broker, accountant, or attorney (or any professional team member) to ensure that they will bring value to your transaction. After all, you are hiring them for advice and counsel, and you want your money's worth.

Being the Leasing Broker

As mentioned earlier, many commercial brokers start in leasing commercial space. It may be retail, office, or industrial space, or a combination. It depends on the size of the market.

To be effective and competent, a broker must know the inventory of space, what terms are being offered, vacancy rates, and overall economic conditions in the market. Trying to keep track of all commercial space in a large market is impossible for one broker, which is why many commercial firms have brokers who specialize. The specialization can be in retail, office, industrial, land, and investment properties. Within those, there are subspecialties. Take retail where subspecialties could include leasing mall space, leasing to anchor tenants or big boxes, shop leasing, single-tenant buildings, and restaurants. In the largest markets, you will see brokers who practice these subspecialties.

Some brokers work exclusively for a building owner, a developer, or a property management company, representing only their properties. Some brokers represent only certain tenants; yet, other brokers represent both landlords and tenants.

Because the key to any broker's success is knowledge of the market, taking on too much can be a very bad idea. All it takes is a transaction gone bad to ruin your reputation, destroy your self-confidence, and drain your bank account. If you realize that you are in over your head, stop! Get help even if it costs you money, and be honest with your client. They will respect you for it.

■ Summary

Leasing is not as easy as it appears. One short lease clause (or one missing) can impact the value of a property or the use of a tenant's space. Knowing the market—including concessions given, upfitting allowances offered, and lease terms important to your client—can make you one of the more successful brokers!

case study   Leasing

Let's practice your knowledge of demographics, key lease terms, and retailing. Because nearly everyone has gone into some type of store, we can relate more easily to retailers.

You are trying to lease the last shop space of 2,000 square feet in your shopping center. Your area is a high demographic area with lots of disposable income. The center's hours are: Monday through Saturday, 10:00 am to 9:00 pm, and Sunday 1:00 to 5:00 pm. The grocery and drugstore are open longer hours. Your shopping center is comprised of the following:

Tenant/Use	Square Feet	Comments
Grocery	37,500	No other grocery allowed in the center
Drugstore	10,500	Can close if grocery does; can sell limited grocery (outparcel) items
Cleaners	1,200	Pickup station only
Nail salon	1,200	No tanning or hair styling done there; exclusive on nails
Hair salon	2,000	Quick-cuts type of place; no nails
Restaurant	2,000	Deli type
Restaurant	1,200	Pizza, eat in and delivery
Restaurant	2,400	Tablecloth restaurant; exclusive on tablecloths
Tanning	1,200	Can't do nails
Videos and related equipment	2,000	Exclusive on video rental and sales
Hardware store	25,000	
Dress store	2,000	
Shoe store	2,000	Ladies shoes
Ice cream parlor	1,200	Ice cream exclusive
Patio furniture	9,000	Exclusive
Vacant	2,000	

This center is in a popular area, and you have many tenants who are interested. The following are your choices:

Tenant/Use	Terms Offered by Tenant
Day spa	$23 per square foot, triple net, $10 per square foot upfitting allowance, plans to do massage, nails, makeup, hair. Experienced operator with other locations. They want to operate Monday through Saturday, 9:00 am–6:00 pm, and serve a nice lunch.
Video arcade	$30 per square foot, triple net, no upfitting allowance. Won't sell videos; just has games to play there. Experienced operator. Customer base is mostly teens.
Produce market	$21 per square foot, triple net, $5 per square foot upfitting allowance; will sell primarily specialty items. New in market, experienced operator.
Bookstore	$25 per square foot, triple net with expense caps; will take space as is; will sell books, newspapers, etc. Requires exclusive. National chain.
Dress store	$32 per square foot, $6 per square foot upfitting allowance, triple net lease. New business. The owner has children in school and wants to operate Monday through Saturday, 10:00 am–4:00 pm.

You want the best tenant for your center and the best deal for the landlord. Analyze the deals offered by the tenants and decide what the issues (if any) are.

_____

_____

_____

_____

_____

■ Review Questions

1. A broker meets with a potential tenant seeking space. The broker interviews the tenant to ascertain needs and wants. The broker needs to know
   a. the amount of space needed.
   b. the type of business.
   c. the amenities needed.
   d. all of these.

2. Rent is quoted as $18 per square feet per year, rentable. The building has a 15% load factor. The tenant needs 2,000 square feet. What is the rent per year?
   a. $30,600
   b. $36,000
   c. $41,400
   d. None of these

3. The tenant pays some or all of the expenses of the property, including but not limited to, utilities, real estate taxes, insurance, common area maintenance, utilities, and repairs. This *BEST* describes which type of lease?
   a. Net
   b. Gross
   c. Percentage clause
   d. Full service

4. The landlord pays all expenses, and the tenant's rent is one set amount that may be subject to increases. This *BEST* describes which type of lease?
   a. Net
   b. Gross
   c. Percentage clause
   d. Ground

5. A landlord (or tenant) needs a broker to help them when
   a. there is no one in their company who understands the real estate process.
   b. they don't know the market well.
   c. they haven't time to do the necessary research.
   d. all of these conditions exist.

10

Development

Your career may start in the commercial development field, or you may enter development through your role as a broker. You may decide to develop for your own account (you keep the development as an investment), or you may develop for others. Even if you are a broker or a property manager and never get into the development business, you need to understand the process the developer uses. After all, you will be part of it, either when selling the land, leasing space to tenants, or selling the development. ■

learning objectives

When you have completed this chapter, you will be able to

■ list development team members,

■ describe the development process,

■ create a pro forma,

■ list the elements of a feasibility study, and

■ compare important characteristics of different product types.

■ Key Terms

feasibility study	highest and best use	pro forma
go dark		

Many developers enter the commercial real estate business in one of the following four ways:

1. They buy or sell for their own account.
2. They start in property management (see Chapter 11).
3. They start in leasing (see Chapter 9).
4. They decide to build on or develop a piece of land or substantially renovate an existing structure.

However they entered the business, new developers all have the same questions. They want to know where to start, who needs to be on their team, what it will cost, where they will get the money, and how much time the development will take.

The Development Process

Every development has the following four components that can occur in any order:

1. Acquiring the land
2. Deciding what to do with the property (office, retail, medical, etc.)
3. Finding financing
4. Finding tenants

Acquiring the Land

Developers looking to acquire a piece of land generally have a development plan or tenant in mind. They know what they want to build and where; they just need the best site available. They know what they can afford to pay and have researched the local land-use issues.

The developer may have used important team members, described below, to help with this acquisition.

Commercial broker.   Referred to in the business as the broker, the commercial broker will be able to provide all of the needed local information: zoning information, land-use policies, economic issues, tax incentives, and political undercurrents, as well as competition, demographics, and compatible uses. The broker should have experience in brokering like-kind transactions.

By careful questioning, the broker will ascertain the developer's exact needs and then look in the market to identify those sites that match those needs. In many cases there may be only a few sites that meet the developer's requirements.

The broker will review the sites with the developer, then upon agreement, pursue those that best meet the needs. Most if not all of these sites may not be listed. The broker will contact the owner to see if the property is for sale. If the owner is amenable, the broker will inquire as to the desired price and terms and establish the broker's compensation. This needs to be in writing. Initially the broker must make disclosure to the owner that the broker is representing a potential buyer and caution the seller to refrain from disclosing anything confidential.

The broker may or may not negotiate on behalf of the developer; it depends on what the developer wishes. Some developers want the broker to perform certain duties, and the developer may perform the rest.

The broker will counsel the developer on

- the best price to pay,
- contract terms to request,
- other sites available,
- zoning issues,
- local politics, and
- competition (existing or rumored).

The broker may perform some of the due diligence items. Due diligence items (discussed in detail in Chapter 4 and Chapter 5) are those things done by a purchaser prior to making a final commitment on a property. Due diligence items might include inspections, rezonings, and securing financing.

Land planner.   To decide the best way to lay out a plan on a site, a developer may bring in an experienced land planner. The land planner may be an architect or engineer who specializes in creating site plans. The land planner may also assist with rezoning, acquiring permits, working with the utility departments, estimating some of the development costs, and answering technical questions. The land planner may also work with the project architects and engineers, especially on larger projects. On smaller projects, the land planner may be the project architect and engineer.

In addition to the right team members, another important factor in acquiring land is a good location. Remember: While location is critical to any real estate, a good retail location may be a poor office location, and vice versa. Visibility may be critical to a shopping center but not important to an industrial facility. Being close to the airport may be the primary concern to a manufacturer, but the highrise office tower needs to be located in a central business district that is seldom near the airport. The primary concerns for site selection for the different commercial uses was covered in Chapter 2.

In Chapters 4 and 5 we listed other things a developer must consider when purchasing land for development.

Deciding What to Do With the Land (Feasibility Studies)

Let's say a developer already has acquired a piece of land. How does that developer make the best use of that land? The principle of **highest and best use** (which was also discussed in Chapter 4) is a development fundamental. What legal and economically feasible use can be made to produce the greatest return to the owner?

When conducting **feasibility studies**, the following are a few things to consider:

- How is the land zoned, and can it be rezoned?
- What is the political climate?
- What is the market? What is a needed product in this market? Office space? Grocery? Warehouses?
- What does the site look like? Is the visibility good? How about access? Is the topography conducive to development (some sites have deep valleys that make them more difficult to develop)?
- Do soil conditions add any constraints?
- Are utilities available in the size and capacity needed?

A negative response on one or some of the above may stop a development or cause more expense or time to be used.

Some of the team members helpful here are described below.

Broker.   While discussed earlier, in this stage the broker may also assist in locating tenants and in advising on market lease terms and on negotiating leases.

Land planner.   As discussed earlier, this team member can help with the layout of the site.

Contractor. The builder can help with specific site issues when pricing the contract. The developer may ask the contractor to value engineer the job, meaning that the contractor is to suggest ways to save money while keeping the project on schedule and maintaining high quality. The contractor may also have some helpful ideas on site layout, tenant contacts, and pricing.

Feasibility analyst. A feasibility analyst is typically a consultant who carefully reviews the proposed development, surveys the market, and produces a report. The report can be extensive or very limited. Items in a feasibility report could include the following:

- Competition
- Local, area, and state economy
- Employment
- Demographics
- Land-use issues
- Costs—construction, soft costs, and costs to market the property
- Financing estimates
- Cash-flow projections
- Profitability analysis
- Tenant mix
- Market absorption

Appraiser. Sometimes a commercial appraiser can perform the feasibility study in the appropriate detail to assist a developer in making a decision. Also the appraiser can help by giving an opinion of value on the land and then on the development when completed. This is usually a necessary step in larger developments when obtaining a loan.

Lender. We discussed financing in greater detail in Chapter 7, but don't underestimate the lender as a resource. Lenders may see many development projects come across their desks, and they have certain insight into the market dynamics of the area. Lenders may be able to assist with cost or income estimates based on what they see in the market.

Attorney. Contrary to public opinion, attorneys who work with developers can truly be deal savers. Experienced real estate attorneys may have suggestions, based on what they have seen on other deals. While the attorney's main role is to limit liability for the developer and to assist on some of the technical aspects of contract negotiation, the savvy attorney should be able to bring other value to the table with thoughtful ideas. Some attorneys may assist in rezonings and tenant negotiations.

Finding Financing

Again, a developer may start with financing—an investor may be anxious to invest in real estate development. Then the developer is in search of a development idea and site.

The more traditional approach is for a developer to have a development in mind, find the land, then seek financing. As shown earlier, the prudent developer has already talked to a lender when deciding on a site or a development plan.

The developer may seek financing from many sources (see Chapter 7 for more information). Financing sources can include the following:

- Developer's own money
- Developer's family's money
- Developer's company funds
- Business associates of developer
- Real estate syndications—placed by investment bankers
- Banks
- Mortgage brokers and mortgage bankers
- Life insurance companies
- Pension funds
- Savings associations
- Individuals seeking investments
- Corporate investors

In order to begin the search for financing, the developer will need to create two pro formas—a cost pro forma and an income pro forma. The cost pro forma will detail the cost and timing of the project. The income pro forma will show the estimated rental income and projected expenses of the completed project.

These pro formas are critical to the lender because the real estate development will be the primary collateral for the loan; in some cases, the real estate may even be the only collateral. The lender must ensure that the property will produce the income forecasted to justify the lender making the loan. The lender must always consider, no matter who the borrower is, "What if we have to foreclose? What price will the foreclosed development bring, and will that price be enough to repay the loan?" The project's riskiest time is during construction, which is why the interest rate is usually a floating rate; the loan is for a short period; and the developer must personally guarantee the construction loan. We'll look at the pro forma again later in this chapter.

The lenders may have preleasing requirements before they commit to and fund a loan, or before they will release the developer from personal guarantees. The terms of a loan will be more attractive if the development is leased than if it is not. If there is no preleasing, it may be referred to as a spec project, meaning that it is speculative and riskier. Financing will be more difficult to obtain and may be unavailable.

Important team members during the preleasing phase are discussed below.

Lender.   A mortgage banker, mortgage broker, or the lender's employee will want to make this loan if it meets the lender's parameters. Consequently, the lender's representative will assist the developer by making suggestions to make the project less risky or more profitable. Suggestions—such as terms in tenant leases, inspections needed, experts to call on (traffic engineers, zoning consultants, marketing gurus)—can make a big difference to a project's success, which is everyone's goal.

Architect, engineer, and land planner.   These team members will assist with the preparation of cost pro formas. When cost-saving or income-producing suggestions are made, redesign might be necessary, and these professionals will be the ones who carry it out.

Finding Tenants

Sometimes a developer has a tenant in hand and is searching for the right land to build a facility. Other times, the developer is developing a concept and is in search for the best tenant.

What makes a tenant a good tenant? In general, there are three things, discussed below, that make a tenant desirable: operating history, financial condition, and business savvy.

Operating history.   A tenant who has successfully operated a business in the recent past has a good track record. It shows the developer and lender important things: The tenant knows how to operate a business, and the tenant has handled their financial obligations properly. From the retail developer's view, it gives some assurance that the tenant won't **go dark**. Going dark means closing the store and discontinuing operations; the front windows are dark because the lights have been turned out. A shopping center developer does not want a store in the shopping center closed. It reduces traffic and makes the center look distressed. Further, depending on the strength of the tenant, the closed store may hurt other tenants' businesses if they relied on the customers from the closed tenant to shop at their store also.

Financial condition.   Besides the obvious need to pay rent and other expenses, lenders base some or all of the lending decision on the financial strength of the tenants. After all, the lender is looking for that tenant rent to continue to produce income and add value to the development. Strong tenant financials and a good operating history allow the lender to offer more attractive loan terms because the loan appears less risky. The relationship between the tenant's strength and the loan terms depends on the size of the development, the size of the tenant, and the strength of the developer.

Business savvy.   This characteristic may seem to be the same as operating history, but there is a subtle difference. Tenants who change with the times, work with the developer to create a better development, and look at the development as a collaborative effort between the developer and the tenants can make a big difference to the success of a development. Tenants who are always complaining, don't provide great customer service, and are behind the times for their business will be a source of irritation for the developer, property manager, and owner.

Checking carefully on each of these three tenant qualities is important because the right tenant can make the deal work, while the wrong tenant can drive the deal into the ground or relegate the deal to mediocre status at best.

In some cases, tenant selection is poorly done due to changes in the market between the initial study and project completion. As payments become due to contractors and lenders, the beleaguered developer feels that any tenant is better than no tenant. While this may be a short-term fix, it has long-term ramifications. Some developments never succeed because a poor tenant mix is difficult to repair.

The team members who assist in tenant qualification and selection are discussed below.

Broker.   The broker can help locate the best tenants for the developer's project. Some brokers specialize in tenant representation—tenant rep—and represent national tenants in specific cities and states. The tenant rep knows the tenant's requirements and approval processes. The tenant rep can move things along quickly by eliminating those sites that don't meet the tenant's specifications and by focusing on those that do.

Brokers who do not specialize in tenant rep work can also be helpful by surveying the market and calling on suitable tenants for the development. The broker needs to clarify whom he or she is representing, the landlord or the tenant. This is discussed in more detail in Chapter 8. Brokers can represent the landlord and call on prospective tenants to encourage them to view the project, or they can represent a variety of tenants who are looking for space.

Tenants. Existing tenants or tenants with whom the developer has a relationship can suggest potential tenants. In retail situations, a major tenant may suggest suitable tenants to compliment the tenant mix. In an office development, a tenant may suggest other firms with whom they do business.

■ Business Climate

At every step in the development process, it is crucial for the developer to understand the area's business climate, in other words, to understand the way things are done in the area. Do the local officials make it difficult to do business? Does development take longer or cost more to build because of this? Is development in this business climate worth it?

Discussed below are some of the business-climate issues to consider.

Obtaining Approvals

Approvals must be obtained for building permits, occupancy permits, and business licenses. Is the process cumbersome in the potential development area? Is there too much red tape and bureaucracy? Are fees high? Is the approval process too uncertain and time-consuming?

Cost Estimates

The same questions should be asked about cost estimates as are asked about obtaining approvals. Additionally, the developer should consider the workforce used. Is it a union area? Is this development competing with many others for the same workers?

Laws, Ordinances, and Policies

Is the area antigrowth or progrowth? Are there impact fees, transfer taxes, or adequate-facilities ordinances? Adequate-facilities ordinances require certain levels to be met before development can proceed, such as enough room in the schools in the case of residential or multifamily development, road capacity, utility capacity for any type of development, clean air and water levels, adequate police and fire protection.

Open space requirements determine how much of a site can be used for development. There may be tree ordinances requiring certain tree protections, prohibiting removal of trees of a certain size and requiring new developments to plant a specified number of trees.

How is storm water handled? Does the government have excessive standards?

Are sign permits difficult to obtain? Are the sign regulations reasonable?

On larger developments, are mixed uses required or encouraged? An example of a mixed use is a development having single-family, multifamily, some retail, and office integrated in the same development. Parking requirements can go both ways—too much or not enough. When an area is promoting more urban, or denser, developments, parking ratios frequently decline. It is assumed that people will walk to the businesses or park their cars on the street, rather than use a large paved parking lot. On some suburban developments, ordinances may require more parking than needed.

With all the facts known (referred to as due diligence) the developer knows whether it's best to move forward or move on.

■ Creating a Pro Forma

When developing a property or redeveloping one, the developer must assemble cost estimates, and that is done with a **pro forma**. We will briefly discuss two pro formas: a cost pro forma (which measures what a development will cost to build) and an income pro forma (which measures the income the development will produce). In Chapter 7, we went into much more detail about pro formas, and we showed sample pro formas in Chapter 6.

The cost pro forma is easy to discuss but sometimes hard to create. The developer must list all expenses. Some items found on a cost pro forma would include the following:

- Land
- Cost of building construction
- Cost to market and lease the property
- Site work and utilities
- Studies required (environmental, traffic study, market analysis)
- Cost of permanent loan (points, origination fee)
- Appraisal
- Architectural
- Engineering
- Landscaping
- Roads
- Cost of construction loan
- Interest during the construction period
- Legal costs

The list can be broad or very detailed. The goal is to list as many known costs as possible to ascertain whether or not it is feasible to develop. For example, if the property costs more to build than it will be worth after completion (based on the income) then why build it? It's just like overimproving a home and then not being able to get out of it what was put into it. In Chapter 7 we analyzed and evaluated some actual numbers.

You might wonder where one can find these numbers. The answer is that you just ask for them. Good sources for these numbers are mortgage bankers who make loans to developers. They see pro formas every day and know what is normal in the market. Another good source can be commercial appraisers. They also work with income properties and know what costs are. Experienced developers use their own experiences coupled with estimates from their team members—contractors, architects, engineers, landscape architects, other developers, bankers, et cetera.

Once costs are estimated, an income pro forma is created. The purpose is to estimate the net operating income (NOI) so that value can be estimated.

To create an income pro forma, the developer will need to compile the following. Note: All numbers are annual numbers. The forecasts may be for several years, so the developer can see how the property matures and estimate the value and projected sales date.

> \+ Gross potential income expected (done from a market study)
> \+ Other income expected (vending income, forfeited deposits, late fees)
> – Vacancy estimated
> – Bad debt expected (there will be some!)
> – Operating expenses
> \+ Reimbursements from tenants
> = Net operating income

From the NOI, the developer will need to deduct capitalized expenses and operating reserves to see the true cash position. Some lenders will deduct reserves from income to derive NOI. As a new developer, be sure to ask about their procedure.

Once the developer knows the NOI, by using market investment rates, such as capitalization rates (see Chapters 6 and 7), the developer can estimate the value of the center and the amount they can expect to borrow from a lender.

What if:

> Cost to build = $5,000,000
>
> Value based on NOI = $4,200,000

Why would a developer want to spend time and energy and have all the risk to build a development worth $800,000 less than it costs? Unless there is some unusual potential for major rent increases or some extraordinary tax credits, it would be folly to continue with this development.

Now, let's flip the numbers:

> Cost to build = $4,200,000
>
> Value based on NOI = $5,000,000

If these numbers are firm, then the developer has just developed a profit of $800,000!

■ Timelines

How long does it take to develop a property? First let's review the following four components to any development:

1. Acquiring the land
2. Deciding the best use of the property
3. Finding financing
4. Finding tenants

Remember that these components can occur in any order. You may already have the land or the tenant or the money. It doesn't matter if it is a 10,000-square-foot drugstore or a million-square-foot mixed-use development. No matter which one of these is your starting point, all the following tasks must eventually be done:

- Negotiating the purchase of the property/land
- Determining best use
- Finding tenants and negotiating with them
- Securing funding

Then the steps in the process tend to be in the following order:

Step 1. Create conception plans.

Step 2. Create final drawings and determine pricing.

Step 3. Select a contractor.

Step 4. Confirm utilities.

Step 5. Secure rezoning.

Step 6. Conduct necessary studies.

Step 7. Close on the financing.

Step 8. Do site work.

Step 9. Construct roads, buildings, etc.

Step 10. Finish work.

Step 11. Close loans and move tenant in.

So the development can take weeks, months, or years. I've always added time to my most conservative schedule and have been glad I did! Ask your team members how long your development should take and have them explain the steps and timeline. We need to know the critical areas. For example, if your grading contractor runs behind, so do you. If the steel contractor is late, you'll have to make up the time somewhere. Other contractors may not be as critical, but at some point, in some way, every contractor will be.

■ Summary

Development is not for the timid. It can be exciting and defeating. A good development never turns out exactly as planned. Opportunities and challenges pop up along the way. The good developer always has a contingency plan ("What will I do if…") and a few spare dollars for those unforeseen challenges (or opportunities).

| case study | **Researching Property** |

A developer has the opportunity to develop a property. He was driving by and saw some land for sale but knows nothing about it except the price. Name five things the developer should consider before proceeding to purchase the property.

_____

_____

_____

_____

_____

■ Review Questions

1. A broker would counsel a developer on all of the following *EXCEPT*
   a. the best price to pay.
   b. contract terms to request.
   c. local politics.
   d. proper corporate structure.

2. When deciding the best use of a property, a developer might perform which type of study?
   a. Feasibility
   b. Due diligence
   c. Environmental
   d. Market

3. Which of the following would be part of a developer's team?
   a. Lender
   b. Attorney
   c. Appraiser
   d. All of these

4. Which of the following is a developer *LEAST* likely to seek financing from?
   a. The developer's own money
   b. Business associates of developer
   c. Banks
   d. The brokerage firm

5. What makes a tenant a good tenant?
   a. Strong financial statement
   b. Experience
   c. Business savvy
   d. All of these

chapter eleven

Property Management

overview

Property management is critical to the long-term success of holding commercial real estate. It is a very different business than development, leasing, or brokerage. **Property management** focuses on the day-to-day operations of the property. The individual property manager is typically salaried, while the property management firm will typically be paid a fee for its services per its property management agreement. The property manager or property management firm may or may not handle the leasing. ■

learning objectives

When you have completed this chapter, you will be able to

■ define key property management activities,

■ list key elements in a property management agreement, and

■ compute a management fee.

■ Key Terms

property management   property management agreement   property manager

■ Who Should Manage My Property?

Owners should ask themselves the following questions to determine if they need a professional **property manager**:

■ Do I know all the laws (local, state, and federal) that affect this property?

■ Am I experienced in managing property of this type?

■ Do I know the rules of thumb for operational expenses?

- Am I willing to keep up with industry trends so the property can be managed effectively?
- Is this the best use of my time?
- Am I the most qualified person to manage this property?
- Will I know what to do if the fire system leaks and floods the building?
- Can I afford time off from my "real job" to deal with tenant repairs, leasing, and the building inspector?
- Do I know my way around city hall?
- Can I handle a tenant eviction?
- Do I know what to look for when reviewing a tenant's records?
- Do I have a professional accounting system, subject to a tenant's audit?
- Do I have competent experienced legal counsel to assist me with lease negotiations, insurance issues, building codes, permits, etc.?
- Do I have relationships with the necessary contractors where I can call them in the middle of the night to handle an emergency?
- Will I have to hire staff to help manage this property? If so, am I knowledgeable in employment law?

If the answers to any of these questions are "no," then the owner most likely needs a professional property manager. Poor property management can cost an owner much in money, time, and the property's value. A broker specializing in property management can use these questions when interviewing a potential owner client.

While doing a lease audit for a client who owns an office building, I noticed that they had not adjusted anyone's rent for several years. The building was 100% occupied and had a waiting list. It was an attractive building in a great location. The leases allowed for a consumer price index (CPI) increase every year and expense pass-throughs. When I asked the owners why they hadn't adjusted anyone's rent, they said they didn't really understand how to do it and were afraid someone might move out. When I pointed out that the building was full and there was a waiting list and that current market rents were higher than the lease rates they were getting, they agreed that I could try to raise the rents but not by the full amount, and I couldn't recoup lost increases from previous years.

I sent rent increase letters to all the tenants and also explained that we'd be doing some expense pass-throughs. We hadn't chosen to do so in the previous years, but we needed to recoup some of the overage now. Effective in 60 days, we would increase their rent by 5% (actually we should have increased rents by over 15%) and we'd be passing through $0.25 per square foot in overages from the previous year, payable in quarterly installments (the lease allowed for a single payment, due within 60 days). To everyone's surprise, no tenants complained, and no one moved out.

How much money do you think this change saved the owner? Well, in round figures:

$0.25 × 50,000 sq. ft. = $12,500 (expense pass-throughs)
5% × $15 × 50,000 sq. ft. = $37,500 (rent increases)
Total = $50,000/yr.

Remember, collecting the rent increase did not require any extra expense, just the time to compute the increases and write the letters.

Besides the extra income, collecting this money added value to the building. While they weren't considering selling, the owners were planning to refinance. Income property is valued on its income (see Chapters 6, 7, and 10). At the time, capitalization rates for office buildings such as this one were 9%. The extra $50,000 increased the value by over $500,000 ($50,000 ÷ 9% = $555,555)!

Keep in mind that because this income was ignored for four years, that money is lost forever. Yes, there are times and circumstances where an owner might want to defer rent increases, but this was not one of them.

A shopping center owner complained that his taxes had gone up and his profitability had decreased. I knew that he was suffering vacancy losses and asked if the tax assessor took that into account. He was clearly confused by my questions. I asked if he had appealed the assessment, and, again, I got a blank look. I asked if his property manager had brought this to his attention, and the owner said that he paid the taxes himself and the property manager didn't have any insight into the tax issues.

I suggested that he contact a tax service to see if an appeal was feasible. Because I had a shopping center nearby, I knew that his taxes were too high. He contacted a tax service that was able to appeal his assessment and reduce his taxes by $17,000 per year. The owner owed a fee to the tax service and to me, but those amounts were small compared to the $17,000 a year he saved.

It's important for a property owner to have someone who looks at these types of things daily and keeps current with the industry trends. A good property manager should save an owner more than the owner pays to that manager in fees.

■ The Property Management Agreement

Most states require a real estate agent to have a written agreement with an owner to manage their property. State laws will dictate some of the requirements, but all **property management agreements** should address the items discussed below.

Agreement Terms

Names.   Owner and agents' names must be accurate.

Property.   Address and description of the property to be managed.

Agent's duties.   List all the duties the agent is to perform and the limit of the agent's authority. Typical duties may include the following:

- Collect rent
- Pay bills
- Evict delinquent tenants
- Handle maintenance and repairs
- Supervise on-site staff
- Prepare reports
- Remit proceeds to owner
- Execute leases (important to stipulate authority)

Note that the property manager is not typically responsible for leasing. It may certainly be added to the agreement, and there may be separate compensation for any leasing activity. On the other hand, an owner may elect to hire another firm to handle the leasing. This division of labor means the two real estate companies (the property management firm and the leasing firm) must coordinate activities to ensure the best for the property.

Agent compensation. State how the agent is to be compensated. Remuneration can be a flat amount per month, a percentage of rents collected, or a combination. Also state how the fee is to be paid and when it is due to the agent.

Sale of property. If the property is to be sold, the selling process will mean extra work for the agent. The property management agreement should address any additional compensation to be paid to the agent for their efforts during a sale.

Term of agreement. When does the agreement begin and end? How are renewals handled? State law may limit options or dictate terms.

Notices. What are the addresses of the property manager (agent) and the owner? In the event that there are multiple owners, the agent should require the owners to select a point person so that the agent isn't receiving conflicting directives.

Bankruptcy, reorganization. Decide what should happen in the event the owner or agent declares bankruptcy or reorganizes.

Records. State where all property records will be kept and spell out the owner's right to inspect. Keep in mind that many tenant leases give the tenant the right to inspect the books if the tenant is responsible for some of the expenses of the property. If there are specific reports to be done by specific dates, that procedure should be stated also.

Insurance. State the dollar amounts and types of insurance to be carried by the owner and the agent. Insurance types typically addressed include the following:

- *Public liability insurance.* This should include property damage and personal injury. It is carried by the owner and, typically, will name the agent as an "additional insured."
- *Comprehensive general liability.* This is usually carried by the agent.
- *Automobile liability.* This is usually carried by the agent.
- *Workers' compensation.* This insurance is usually carried by the entity that hires the employees.

Compliance with legal requirements. How will required compliance issues be handled? For example, suppose the town ordinance was changed and required that all signage be changed to meet new height restrictions. How should that be handled and by whom?

As with the other two contracts discussed in Chapter 5, there are other clauses necessary for the protection of the parties (e.g., signature blocks, miscellaneous, parties, and benefit). An experienced property manager or real estate attorney will be able to add those clauses necessary for the particular property.

■ Getting Paid

How much should a property manager charge to manage a property? It depends on several variables. Fees are highly negotiable, but there are rules of thumb in each specialty.

Let's look at it from the owner's point of view first. The property can afford only so much overhead. As stated earlier, the property manager's expertise should make the owner more money (or at least as much money) as the fee. A small property or one that produces little income cannot afford to pay much. However, this property may take as much time and effort to manage as a larger property. It's a matter of economics.

The fee can be a percentage of rents, a flat amount, or some combination of the two. For example, let's say a property has gross rents of $13,000 per month. Let's say our fee agreement is 4% of gross rents or $500 per month, whichever is greater. The property management fee for the month would be $520 ($13,000 × 4% = $520). The percentage or flat fee amounts and the way gross rents are defined are negotiable.

Something else to determine when agreeing to a fee is what the property will pay and what the property manager will pay. For example, who pays the property manager's expenses when visiting a property? Who pays the bookkeeping expenses? That little $520 per month fee can be quickly eaten up by travel expenses and personnel costs if they are to be borne by the property manager.

Now, let's look at it from the property manager's view. The property manager must consider how much time, effort, and expense it will take to successfully and competently manage the property. Sometimes, it's just not worth it. Sometimes, though, a property manager will accept a property to manage with the hopes of getting other (more profitable) properties to manage from the same owner.

My property management firm took a small, unprofitable shopping center to manage that was an hour and a half from our office. Because we didn't have any other property in that direction, property visits and meetings took most of a day when the travel was considered. In addition, there was the cost of travel and the additional liability of driving the distance. While we had some familiarity with the area, we didn't know as much as we needed to know. Consequently, we spent valuable time getting to know the town, the politics, and the contractors. We lost money on the management of this center and it was a constant nightmare—maintenance issues, tenant problems, etc. Why did we take the job? Because it was part of a large and profitable portfolio of property we were managing.

After six months of managing this center, we decided to cut our losses and, with the permission of the owner, contracted with another firm to manage it locally. We continued to supervise it, but the day-to-day efforts were handled by folks who knew the area. While we continued to lose money on this center's management, we more than made up for it with the other properties.

■ Typical Day of a Property Manager

The best way to learn about the day-to-day tasks of a property manager is to look at an example. The following is a recounting of a typical day of an office building property manager. I admit that I embellished this a bit for entertainment value. However, I have had days very similar to this!

8:00 am   You arrive on-site. Tour the outside of the property and make a to-do list for the landscapers and maintenance crew. You notice a missing sprinkler head, and water is shooting up across the sidewalk (again). As you get ready to walk inside, a tenant asks you when you will be replacing the broken glass. You ask, "What broken glass?" And the tenant points up. You note that a large panel of glass is shattered between the second and third floors. You make a note.

8:15 am   You tour the inside of the building, checking restrooms and storage areas. Make appropriate lists.

8:40 am   The maintenance supervisor has tracked you down, explains he needs supplies that day (and needs a purchase order now), and informs you that the central heating, ventilation, and air-conditioning (HVAC) unit is "acting odd." He will follow up and let you know.

8:45 am   When you return to your office, you find 12 phone messages on your desk that were not there before (you've been gone 30 minutes!). Your cell phone has gone off 10 times this morning. You call the glass company about the shattered panel on the front of your building. They will call back with a quote and an appointment time.

9:30 am   You return calls, complete the needed purchase order for supplies, and call the HVAC service company because your maintenance supervisor has called to say the systems now "smell funny" and you'd "better get someone out there." You've noticed that it feels warm in your office, and the TV weather forecaster predicted the high to be in the 90s today.

Your phone is ringing with tenants calling to say that a large tree limb has just fallen, hitting a car, and has blocked a driveway.

10:00 am   You've now investigated the tree limb, called the insurance company, had your administrative assistant (admin) find out whose car was damaged, and called the tree folks to come out and remove the limb (size of a telephone pole) and give you an estimate of the cost to take down the tree that the limb fell from. You can see other limbs ready to fall.

10:20 am   You return to your office where there are another 12 phone messages on your desk along with the tenant whose car was damaged by the limb. She is very upset because her car is only two months old. She's not sure her insurance will cover it. On a positive note, the glass company has left a message that they are on their way. You return calls and field calls from tenants who "smell something funny" and are hot.

10:45 am   The glass people, the tree company, your insurance agent, and the HVAC folks arrive at exactly the same time. You look for your admin, but she is out dealing with a new tenant who moved in over the weekend and has discovered that the outlets aren't working properly (they were when you checked them out Friday). You call your maintenance supervisor; he is at the hardware store picking up needed supplies. You dispatch the glass folks to repair the panel, the tree folks to remove the branch and get an estimate for removing the tree, and the HVAC folks to check out the smell and lack of air-conditioning.

You sit down with your insurance agent who informs you that your deductible is probably larger than the claim, and besides it does not cover damage to cars unless they are owned by the development. He plans to file a report anyway and confides to you that the rates for your entire company will likely increase and maybe some of the buildings will have their insurance canceled.

11:00 am The fire alarm goes off because the HVAC folks got too close to a sensor with a torch. They quickly silence it, but the fire department is on their way. The fire department arrives. You wave them off, but they are required to check the building and reset the fire-alarm system. While the fire marshal is working his way to the equipment room, he notices that the building's fire extinguisher is not properly charged. A citation is written and handed to your insurance agent because the fire marshal has confused the agent with property management staff. Your insurance agent is writing something in his notebook, looking at the citation. He hands the citation to you.

11:30 am The glass folks have removed the panel only to discover that the one they brought is not the correct size or color. After several phone calls to their office, they inform you that your panel is special-order spandrel glass. Not only will it cost five times what you expected, it will take six weeks to arrive. You instruct the glass company to install, in the meantime, whatever they have on hand, knowing it won't match the surrounding glass.

11:45 am The tree people come in to say they have removed the limb, but it poked a large hole in your asphalt and damaged your Dumpster fence. While the tree itself is not yet dead, it is in poor health. But, it is a protected species and cannot be removed without a special permit. To get the permit, you need to call the one person in your ten-county area who can certify that this tree is a goner and get his opinion. He is on vacation. There are two other limbs that look dangerous, and they can be removed for $13,000. You figured less than that to remove the entire tree. Because you cannot move ahead without other bids, you send them on their way.

12:00 pm The building is warmer, and the smell is stronger. You look for the HVAC workers and are told that they are at lunch.

While you are walking down the hall toward your office, a tenant races out of the men's room saying that a commode is overflowing. You dash in and turn off the water to that commode. You call your janitorial staff and report water on the floor. You mark the commode "out of order" and make a note for your maintenance staff. Your janitor stops by your office to say that the water is mopped up and the rest of the plumbing seems to be working OK.

12:30 pm The fire marshal informs you that all your fire extinguishers are discharged and your fire door was propped open again, and that is a serious violation. He will now do a full inspection.

A prospective tenant walks in, asking for the leasing agent. Apparently they have a 12:30 pm appointment. Because you can't find the leasing agent, you begin a tour of the building with the prospect. The agent takes over when she arrives 15 minutes later.

1:00 pm The new tenant still can't get the outlets working and says that due to this malfunction, the heat, and the smell, he cannot do any business; his secretary has gone home with a headache; and he wants a rent abatement. He's on the top floor where the smell and the heat are the strongest. You go up there to appease him. When you get into his space, you notice a stain on the ceiling tile and figure that the HVAC workers must have ripped a condensation line and caused some water to run into the ceiling. You make a note to have staff replace the ceiling tile ASAP.

1:30 pm When you return to your desk, you find a message from the press who want to know if you had a building fire because one of their reporters heard the call over the radio. You also see a message from yesterday stuck to a file folder. It's from the Chicago asset manager of your owner requesting a budget update ASAP for a 2:00 pm (CT) meeting today. Because you are on ET, you have 1½ hours to get this update done and emailed. This should not be a problem. Your admin can do this as you just updated everything last week.

1:45 pm   Your admin is updating the numbers. You expect her to be finished by 2:15 pm at the latest.

2:15 pm   Your admin tells you she is done and has emailed the update to your asset manager. Five minutes later, your asset manager calls for the budget update, and you tell her that it's been emailed. She tells you that the corporate server is down due to a virus and asks if you could you fax it.

2:30 pm   Your asset manager calls to say she got it, "thanks," but her meeting was postponed until next week. Can you update it again then?

2:30 pm   Your maintenance supervisor comes into your office and suggests you sit down. He tells you that the fire marshal tripped over the HVAC guys' equipment and sprained his ankle. You need to call the insurance agent. The HVAC system is probably OK—they think it's just a connection and a software issue. You remember about the stained ceiling tiles on the top floor. You ask him to replace them today. It seems to be getting cooler. The smell is gone and so is the fire truck. You start to assemble the files you need for an upcoming three-day management meeting.

2:45 pm   Your maintenance supervisor returns to your office, and he is all wet. He suggests you sit down. When he removed the water-stained ceiling tiles, quite a bit of water poured down into the tenant's computer station. He says there was a lot of water in the ceiling area. Seems another branch from the (now protected) tree must have blown down last night during the storm and punched a hole in your roof membrane. It's a mess. You call the roof contractor. You call the tree guys. You call your insurance agent. You put them on speed dial as you think you'll be calling them again soon.

3:15 pm   As you are leaving the office to pick up a late lunch, you notice the front of your building in your rearview mirror. The glass contractor used a piece of plywood to replace the shattered glass. It looks terrible. You call your maintenance supervisor to get him to deal with this, and he tells you that the glass people don't have any spandrel glass in stock large enough to fit. You ask him to call other glass companies. He says he has and we are just out of luck. Plywood will have to do unless you'd prefer fiberboard.

3:30 pm   While eating, you are putting together your report for the three-day meeting that begins tomorrow afternoon. Like a bolt of lightning, you remember the insurance issues and the fire marshal's citations. You call your supervisor and leave a detailed voice mail and call back to have your admin fax everything to your corporate office in Atlanta. As required, you also leave a voicemail for the asset manager in Chicago who promptly phones you on your cell phone. She asks if you've completed the required "incident reports." You confess that you haven't, explaining that it's been a particularly hectic day. Can they wait? She is sympathetic but says the reports need to be filed within 24 hours of the incidents. You promise you'll send the reports before tomorrow morning.

4:30 pm   As you finish your reports, you see that you have 14 messages on your phone. You start listening to your messages.

The fire marshal is OK; his ankle is strained, not sprained. He'll be back tomorrow to finish the inspection. He's not found anything serious except the discharged extinguishers and propped open door. The door was propped open by the HVAC guys who have gotten him to remove that from his report.

The roof contractor has patched the holes in the membrane. There is a lot of water in the ceiling and they suggest with the warm weather, you might have a problem with mold and you need to get it dried out soon. You call your maintenance supervisor to handle it. You make a note to climb into the ceiling area to have a look yourself.

The tree contractor has removed the branch on the roof and hauled it off. They think they can now justify taking the tree down without the letter from the specialist. They quote an acceptable price. You call your maintenance supervisor and tell him to tell them to proceed while you are gone.

Your insurance agent says that nothing that happened today will affect your insurance. However the damaged car is not covered.

Your maintenance supervisor leaves a message that the commode is fixed.

4:45 pm When you return to the property, you notice the plywood on the window again. You are determined to get something else. You call your maintenance supervisor and have him meet you in your office. You are nearly prepared for the meeting the next day. You ask your maintenance supervisor to do something about the plywood and the hole in the asphalt that the branch made. That needs repair as does the Dumpster fence. Your maintenance supervisor says he will have everything done within the next few days. He's also run out to the hardware store again to get batteries and new fire extinguishers. The old ones were defective and wouldn't hold a charge. They were charged only a month ago. When the fire marshal returns the next day, he will see charged extinguishers. He may elect to tear up today's citations.

5:30 pm You have returned all your calls, inspected the roof and ceiling, completed the incident reports, and gotten the mail ready to take out. Looks like you won't have to come back in tonight.

While this may not be a typical day, any experienced property manager will tell you that they have had a day or two similar to this. The property manager wears many hats. Depending on the size of the staff, the property manager may wear all of the hats. While no one is an expert at everything, the property manager may be required to use outside contractors for everything and, therefore, be a coordinator of services.

The property manager may also handle marketing and leasing. While it is not unusual for a company to have someone else handle the leasing besides the property manager, it will depend on the talents and the agreements.

Following is a summary of what we saw the property manager do:

- Inspect the property
- Supervise staff
- Contract with subcontractors
- Handle an insurance claim
- Deal with upset tenants
- Work with regulatory officials
- Handle property damage
- Spot a water leak
- Prepare reports for owner
- Use technology
- Work with a prospective tenant
- Coordinate with leasing staff
- Routine office duties
- Handle emergency and nonemergency repairs and maintenance, such as cutting off the water to an overflowing commode, a task every property manager knows how to do

Many days on-site may be much more routine. Then there are the days when the property manager is responding to an event or crisis (fire, flood, accident). In some cases the property manager may not know of a problem until long after it has occurred. In that case, the property manager will deal with the insurance company and "clean up the mess."

A property manager's job is both proactive and reactive. It can be a very demanding job, but it is never dull!

One of the things we didn't see in the earlier scenario is the duty of rent collection and lease enforcement. Again, according to the property management agreement, the property manager might have the duty to collect and account for property rents and might be the party who verifies and pays the property's expenses. In that case, it is likely that the management company is responsible for preparing and tracking the property's operating budget. The management company may also be charged with implementing the property's capital improvements program.

■ Summary

The illustration of a property manager's typical day may have some extremes, but it was meant to entertain as well as educate. Many of the day-to-day duties were shown, but hopefully no property manager has all those things happen in one day! Decisions made by the property manager affect the financial success of the building owner and the tenants of the property. Poor decisions can give rise to lawsuits, property damage, violations of ordinances and codes, and just bad business. It takes a special type of real estate professional to successfully manage all of the requirements that a property presents.

case study — Property Management

1. Name at least five things property managers may do in their day-to-day business.

   Deal w/ tenants.
   Property issues.
   Damaged caused to personal property while on site.
   Collect rents.

2. As the property manager, you continue to struggle with getting the landscaping contractor to service your property on a timely basis. Frequently, the grass is overgrown or the shrubs need trimming. For this reason, your employers are considering hiring an employee to handle the bulk of the grounds work when the contractor's contract expires. You can still contract for any large jobs, if needed. List the pros and cons of having an employee versus using an outside contractor.

	Employee	Contractor
Pros	*Timely response to landscaping*	*No loaded cost.*
Cons	*Loaded cost Ins, Payroll, Unemployment benefits*	*Shit service.*

■ Review Questions

1. Which of the following duties would a property manager most likely *NOT* perform?

    a. Collect rent

    b. Arrange for repairs

    c. Handle the owner's income taxes

    d. Prepare reports for the owner

2. A property management agreement would *NOT* address which of the following items?

    a. Handling of repairs

    b. Refinancing of the development

    c. Authority of the property manager

    d. Compensation

3. Reports done by the property manager are specified by whom?

    a. Owner, per the property management agreement

    b. Local, state, and federal requirements

    c. Property management company

    d. All of these

4. Which of the following is a question an owner should ask to determine whether a property manager is needed?

    a. Do I know all the laws (local, state, and federal) that affect this property?

    b. Do I know the rules of thumb for operational expenses?

    c. Is this the best use of my time?

    d. All of these

5. If the property management fee is the higher of 5% of gross receipts or $1,200 per month and gross receipts are $32,000 per month, what is the fee for that month?

    a. $1,200

    b. $1,500

    c. $1,600

    d. $2,000

Due Diligence Checklist

Because it is easy to overlook confirmation of certain facts when working on a project, it always helps to have a checklist. A checklist is especially useful and important if several people are working on the same project. Each person may assume another person is handling a task when in fact no one is.

Not all of these checklist items will be applicable to every development, and there may be some things needing to be addressed that are not on this checklist.

Zoning/Planning/General Development Policies

- In what jurisdiction is the development?
- Are there annexation plans?
- What is current zoning?
- What does city or county want there?
- Exactly what will it allow?
- Is there a sunset clause or amortization on current use?
- Is current use legal?
- Can use be changed?
  - To what?
- What zoning is needed?
- What is the process?
- Can expansions and/or renovations be done?
- What is the rezoning process?
- How much does rezoning cost?
- Will the timing work?
- What is likelihood of rezoning?
- Are there local issues such as politics?
- Are there any conditional zoning requirements?
- Will special permits be needed?
- What is the permit process?
- What are the buffer requirements?

- Are sizes for berms specified?
- Are there any moratoriums in place or expected?
- What is the subdivision process?
- Is there a sign ordinance?
- What signage is allowed?
- How are permits handled?
- What triggers a permit?
- What laws, acts, local ordinances, or policies affect this property?
- Does the Coastal Area Management Act (CAMA) apply?
- Does the Mountain Ridge Act apply?
- What are the watershed regulations?
- What are the wetlands rules?
- What are the lake setback regulations?
- Are there any smart growth policies?
- Any general development policies in place?
- Is any of the property in the floodplain or flood fringe?
- How current are the floodplain maps?

Site Issues

- Do you know the exact size and shape of the site?
- Are surveys available?
- How current are the surveys?
- Has any of the site been sold off since the last survey?
- What is the timing in getting a current survey?
- Are there any encroachments?
- Does anything look close to encroaching?
- Which of the following types of survey are needed?
    - Boundary?
    - Location?
    - Topographical?
    - Subdivision?
    - Construction?
    - American Land Title Association (ALTA)?
- Are there any easements?
    - Are easements shown on the survey?
    - Can the easements be moved?
    - What is the process, time, and cost involved?
    - How does easement affect land use?
    - Which of the following types of easements are present?
        - Power?
        - Gas?
        - Telecommunications?
        - Drainage?
        - Water?

- Sewer?
- Cable TV?
- Municipal and public?
- Access?
- Greenway?
- Private?
- Access?
- Which of the following best describes the status of the easements?
  - Recorded?
  - Not recorded but suspected or visible?
- Are there any rights-of-way and which of the following describes them?
  - Recorded?
  - Not recorded?
- Do transitional rights-of-way exist?
- Is there additional land taking for slope of road, bridge, etc.?
- Do any of the following local and state transit issues exist?
  - Transit overlay zoning or additional requirements?
  - Road improvement programs?
  - Planned median additions?
  - Elimination of median cuts planned?
- Do any of the following environmental issues exist?
  - Environmental study or studies done?
  - Wetlands?
  - Watershed?
  - Local issues?
  - Drainage policies?
  - Has anyone looked at the property during and after hard rain?
- Are any of the following legal and title issues a problem?
  - Title policy available?
  - Last updated?
  - Exceptions? (Schedule B)
  - Verified?
  - Legal description?
  - Legal access verified?
  - Deed restrictions?
  - Uses restricted?
- Do subdivision issues exist, such as the following?
  - Setbacks?
  - Approvals needed?
  - From whom?
  - Restrictive covenants?
  - POA/HOA (property owner association/homeowners association) details?
  - Enforceable?

- Violated?
- Architectural review committee?
  - Who?
  - How?
  - What are the issues?
- Do any of the following problems exist with the taxing authority?
  - Back taxes paid?
  - Assessment amount and rate?
  - City?
  - County?
  - School district?
  - Utility district?
  - Special taxing district?
  - Are there special assessments?
- What are the assessment policies and methods?
  - Protest procedures?
  - Next valuation?
  - When?
  - What's the word on the streets?
- Has anyone interviewed seller for property history?
- Who provides the following services? Additional costs?
  - Police?
  - Fire?
  - Emergency?
  - Garbage?
  - Other?
- Any mineral rights issues?
- Is visibility a concern?
- Has anyone announced any changes?

Building Code/Development Issues

- Which building code is used?
- What is the local process when building, repairing, or renovating?
- Are moratoriums in place?
- What are the buffer requirements? (see Zoning)
- Is a change of use permit required?
- What are the subdivision regulations?
  - What triggers them?
  - What is the process?
  - What is the timing?
  - What is the cost?
- Are there any submission requirements?
- Are there any political or local issues?

- Are utilities nearby?
  - Availability?
  - Cost?
  - Process?
  - Timetable?
  - Political issues?
  - Anyone who can share installation cost?
  - Reimbursable to installer (developer)?
- What utilities are needed?
  - Power?
  - Water?
  - Sewer?
  - Cable TV?
  - Telecommunications?
  - Wireless service?
  - Gas?
  - Moratoriums?
- Are the soils suitable?
  - Test results?
  - Soils suitability analysis?
  - Compaction?
  - Percolation?
  - Drainage
  - Cost to fix any problems?
  - Rock reported in area?
- What is the vegetation on the property?
  - Existing versus desired?
  - Process and permits?
- Local issues?
  - Are these "dry" counties or towns? (Dry areas are those that don't sell beer, wine, or alcohol. Knowing this is important for restaurants and grocery stores.)
- How much of the site is usable or buildable?
- Is green space required?
- Are height limitations in place?
- Are view corridors required?
- What are the impervious area limitations, if any?
- What do the surrounding properties look like?
- Are roads a consideration?
  - Capacity?
  - Are accel/decel (acceleration/deceleration) lanes required?
  - Are turning lanes required?
  - Is there a sidewalk requirement?
- What endangered and protected species laws apply?

Existing Structure Issues

- Is there an existing structure compliance problem?
- Are copies of original permits available?
- Are permits in place for all alternations?
- Is everything compliant with the Americans with Disabilities Act (ADA)?
- What, if any, are the fire code issues?
- Does everything comply with current building codes?
  - Is anything nonconforming?
  - Is there an amortization period?
  - Is there a sunset clause?
  - What will trigger bringing property into compliance?
  - Is the property's signage legal?
  - What happens when ownership changes?
  - What happens if use changes?
- Proper permits in place for tenant's use?
- Are there any health code issues?
- Are there any environmental issues?
- Must tenant approve sale?
- Any rights of first refusal? Options?
- Is property inspection needed?
  - Done by whom?
- What is the condition of the exterior?
  - Parking lots?
    - ADA compliant?
    - Meet code and zoning regulations?
    - Big enough?
    - Pavement?
    - Striping?
    - Traffic patterns?
    - Site entrances?
    - Loading areas?
    - Dumpster pads and trash areas?
  - Signage?
  - Landscaping?
  - Outside irrigation?
  - Sidewalks?
  - Curb and gutter?
  - Retention or detention ponds?
  - Fenced?
  - Safety hazard?
  - Health issues?
  - Lighting?
  - Utilities visible?
  - Location of fire hydrants?

- Who is responsible for maintenance of the following?
  - Roof?
    - Type?
    - Condition?
    - Warranty?
  - Building exterior (siding)?
    - Glass?
    - Windows?
    - Flashing?
    - Curtain wall?
    - Parapet?
    - Foundation?
    - Soffit vents?
    - Gutter and downspouts?
  - Building entrances?
    - ADA removal of barriers?
    - Thresholds?
    - Doors?
    - Walk-off mats?
    - Locks?
    - Security system?
    - Smoking urns?
    - Alarms?
      - Fire?
      - Theft?
      - Other?
  - Building interior?
    - Interior lighting?
    - Emergency lighting?
  - Ambient lighting?
  - Bulbs and grid condition?
  - Standard-size fixtures that are easily replaced?
  - Ceiling?
    - Grid?
    - Panels?
      - Size, type, and can they be easily replaced?
    - Signs of leaks?
    - Plenum area?
      - Overhead sprinklers, grills, ducts, vents?
    - Signs of damage?
  - Flooring?
    - Carpet condition?
    - Hardwoods?
    - Vinyl?

- Stone?
- Other?
- Elevators?
    - When inspected last?
    - Type?
    - Speed?
    - Capacity?
    - Maintenance contract expiration?
    - Condition?
- Exterior doors and lobby area?
- Stairs?
    - Signage?
    - Treads?
    - Lighting?
    - Doors?
- Fire extinguishers?
    - Number required?
    - Location?
    - Charged?
- Building signage condition?
    - ADA compliant? Braille?
    - Tenant's signage?
    - Lobby?
    - Directionals?
    - Emergency?
- Restrooms?
    - Location?
    - Adequacy and number?
    - Condition?
        - Sinks?
        - Floor?
        - Commodes?
        - Hardware?
        - Floor drains?
        - Mirrors?
        - Paper towel holders?
        - Stalls?
    - ADA compliant?
    - Signage?
    - Evidence of plumbing leaks?
- Mechanical rooms?
    - What's in them?
    - Who has access to them?

- Telecommunications rooms?
  - Condition?
  - Access?
  - Policies?
  - Sufficient for tech needed?
- Maintenance engineer shop?
- Janitorial closets?
- Storage areas?
  - What is stored?
  - Adequate inventory of long lead-time items?
- Pay phones?
  - ADA compliant?
- Tenant spaces?
  - Upfitting financed?
  - Fixtures financed?
  - Appear to comply with (building and zoning) codes?
  - Common areas shared by tenants?
    - Mail?
    - Storage?
    - Concession?
    - Other?
  - Attic?
    - Signs of asbestos?
    - Pest infestation?
    - Insulation?
  - Lobby?
    - Appearance?
    - Finishes?
    - Directory?
    - Furniture?
  - Mechanical Systems?
    - Heating and air-conditioning (HVAC)?
      - Controls?
      - System?
      - Condition?
      - Maintenance records?

Transactional/Business Issues

- Are any of the following approvals needed to close sale?
  - Deed restrictions?
  - Any rights of first refusal?
  - Confirm true ownership and right to contract?
- Does lis pendens exist?
- Are there any red flags?

- Rumors of any kind about the property?
- Is there an existing loan on the property?
  - Is it prepayable?
  - Terms?
  - Cost?
  - Timing?
  - Is it assumable?
- Is an appraisal available? Date?
- Is an appraisal required?
- Are there any insurance issues?

Financial Issues

- Are there any existing loans? (See Transactional/Business issues.)
- Do unrecorded leases exist?
- Is there a pro forma?
  - Current?
  - Feasible?
- Has a lease audit been taken?
  - Tenant's right to cancel lease?
  - Tenant's right to sublet or assign?
  - Credit of major tenants today?
  - Right to go dark?
  - Operating hours?
  - Continuous operation?
  - Noncompete clauses (both landlord and tenant)?
  - Enforcement (or lack of) of lease provisions?
- Are there any reimbursables?
  - What?
  - When?
  - How?
- Do special tenant requirements exist?
  - Parking?
  - HVAC?
  - Metering?
  - Cleaning?
  - Trash?
  - Right of first refusal?
  - Expense stops?
  - Assignable leases?
  - Estoppels required? Available?
- Are expenses as anticipated?
  - Contracts?
    - Expiration?
    - In whose name?

- Has square footage been confirmed?
    - How is space measured?
    - What do the tenant leases say?

Market Issues

- What is market position of subject property?
    - Possibility of repositioning?
- What is market position of surrounding properties?
    - Current uses?
    - "Word on the street" regarding them?
    - Zoning?
- What is the market competition?
    - Recent comps?
    - Status of comps?
- What is the local economy like?
    - Current status and proposed changes?
    - Major industries?
    - Government?
    - Financial issues?
    - Politics?
    - Other local issues?
- What is the condition of the roads?
    - Current?
    - Planned?
    - New roads?
    - Traffic counts?
    - Major corridors?
- Have interviews been done with those "in the know"?
    - Owner?
    - Adjacent property owners?
    - Old-timers?
    - Planning, zoning, and building code officials?
        - Deals permitted?
        - Deals announced?
        - Deals rumored?
    - Elected officials?
    - Tenants?
- What are the demographics?
    - Current?
    - Projections?
    - Trade area?
- Are there other developments in the area?
- What is the location of amenities?
    - Restaurants?

- Residential?
- Hospitals?
- Shopping?
- Education?
- Arts?

Personal Issues

- Are there any personal issues with the buyer or seller?
  - Reputation?
  - Motivation?
- Who are the brokers involved?
  - Reputation?
  - Competence?
- Does buyer or seller own other properties?
  - Next door?
  - Close?
  - Restrictions?
- Are there any warranties and indemnifications?
  - Financial stability?
  - Can the buyer and seller close?
  - Willingness to creatively structure?

If seller:

- When acquired?
- Price and terms?
- Why selling?

If buyer:

- What recently bought?
- Price and terms?

Chapter 1 Case Study Answers

1. Your expertise could be finance, hospitality, restaurants, retail, and more.
2. Whom you know might get you started. If you can't think of a person, you should start your career where you'll be supplied with products or leads.
3. If you need a steady income, try property management. If you need income now, consider working for the government or find a position that is salaried working for an owner.
4. Don't count on your brokerage firm to handle your training. You need to ask yourself and any potential brokers how you can be positioned to succeed.
5. You should understand what attracts you to the commercial real estate field so that you can be sure to work in the area that you enjoy.
6. Just because the trade magazines say real estate is a good investment is not reason enough to get involved in commercial real estate.
7. What type or types of real estate do you relate to? Retail? Office? The better you understand it, the better you can analyze it. Never invest in something you don't understand.
8. Do you have a good broker, accountant, or investment advisor? If you are not a real estate expert, you must have good advisors.
9. Your broker will need to know your source of funds from the start. It makes a difference which deals you are shown.
10. If you have children getting ready for college and you need the money, make sure you are in short-term investments. Always give your broker this kind of information.
11. No one wants to lose money, but let your broker know if you need safer investments. If the loss from an investment would cause serious financial strain, then you need to rethink that investment.
12. You should plan out how much income you expect, when you expect it, how long you will hold the investment, and so on. Again, your broker needs to know this before showing you any property.
13. In determining goals, be sure to have a good advisor. Consider whether your advisor will track your investments for you or whether you plan to do it. If you are not yet an expert, you should ask your advisor to do this.

Chapter 1 Review Questions Answers

1. **d.** All of these. You need to consider how much you know and if the income will be sufficient.
2. **c.** The purpose of an informational interview is for you to get information.
3. **d.** All of these and more are differences.
4. **a.** It's best to send a written "thank you" note. If you know that the interviewer operates best over email, however, you should adjust accordingly.
5. **d.** Many commercial properties may not be in the MLS.

Chapter 2 Case Study Answers

1. Easy to find, near good neighborhood, pleasant setting, near employees' homes.
2. Easy ingress and egress, visibility, parking.
3. Status location, amenities both near and in the building, government incentives, proximity to workforce.
4. Security, proximity to workforce, ingress and egress, tax incentives. There could certainly be more responses, depending on the exact needs, wants, and goals of the user. A credit card processing center could want their location hidden or very visible. Overall, you can see that different users have different requirements. The best way to know exactly what a user needs and wants is to ask them, then qualify their response.

Chapter 2 Review Questions Answers

1. **b.** The retailer needs to know the location of its customers.
2. **c.** The credit card facility is not open to the public and doesn't need to be visible.
3. **a.** An FTZ offers incentives to manufacturers.
4. **c.** A highrise is at least seven stories, usually 10 or more. A five-story building would typically be classified as a midrise. However, real estate is local, so use what is typical in the area.
5. **b.** Because people typically buy bagels for breakfast, the "going toward work" side of the street would be more convenient.

Chapter 3 Case Study Answers

Possible answers include the following four:

1. Do nothing.
2. Sell and reinvest in other property or other investments.
3. Sell and offer seller financing.
4. Do a 1031 exchange.

Chapter 3 Review Questions Answers

1. **b.** A build to suit is built to meet the specifications of the user.
2. **c.** A 1031 exchange, if appropriate and done properly, can defer taxes to a later date.
3. **a.** A sale-leaseback allows the owner to receive money to use to invest in his or her business. The owner can stay in the facility and pay rent.
4. **b.** Real estate is not a liquid investment. If the money will be needed in a short period of time, then real estate may not be the safest investment.
5. **a.** High leverage means a high loan-to-value ratio, low equity.

Chapter 4 Case Study Answers

Attributes	Apartment	Shopping Center	Office
Great visibility	X	X	
On a bus line			X
In a desirable school district	X		
On the "going toward home" side of the road		X	
Fairly flat site			X
In a foreign trade zone (FTZ)			

Chapter 4 Review Questions Answers

1. **c.** In a busy city, the cell company would most likely need to locate their tower on another's building and lease or buy the air rights to do so.
2. **d.** The farmer would be interested in the water rights because it pertains to irrigating his fields.
3. **a.** The fence is encroaching on your property.
4. **b.** You would grant the power company an easement to use a piece of your property for that specific use.
5. **d.** You would do all of these tests and more.

Chapter 5 Case Study Answers

1. Cabbage Corners: $32 + $1 + $0.50 + $1.10 + $0.25 = $34.85 × 1,700 sq. ft. = $59,245. North Street Market: $27 + $1.75 + $0.35 + $0.95 = $30.05 × 1,400 sq. ft. + $42,070. But remember there is some upfitting she will have to pay, and the CAM and real estate taxes at Cabbage Corners are surer than those at North Street Market area. For example, at North Street Market, let's say taxes rise by 30%. That would increase her add on by $0.29 × 1,400 = $406. Let's say CAM goes up $0.25. That increase = $0.25 ×1400 = $350. If she needs to spend $18,000 to finish her space, she needs only $1,000 extra on Cabbage Corners but $18,000 at North Street Market (that is offset by her one month free rent of $3,150, so she needs a net of $14,450).

2. Cabbage Corners has higher household (HH) income because of an adequate number of households (HHs) nearby.

3. North Street Market allows three-year to five-year initial term and options. Cabbage Corners offers no options. She needs to decide which is more important to her business.

4. $27 × 1,400 ÷ 5% = $756,000

5. Cabbage Corners:

   Advantages
   - Specialty center
   - New, items probably under warranty
   - Larger space
   - Higher HH income
   - Fixed CAM
   - Real estate taxes just adjusted
   - Marketing program
   - Upfitting allowance almost covers expense

- Hours of operation better meet a decorating store typical hours
- Days required to be open better meet her needs
- No percentage rent
- Fixed increases
- No spouse cosign needed

Disadvantages

- Space larger and narrower than desired
- Rent higher
- Insurance and real estate tax higher
- Very small center
- Only three-year lease offered and no options
- Marketing assessment may not be well used (spent on efforts not helpful to all tenants)

North Street Market:

Advantages

- Larger center to better spread expenses
- Space more square
- Good HH income and number of HH nearby
- Lower rent
- Lower real estate tax and insurance
- No marketing assessment
- Grocery store and drugstore may provide foot traffic and visibility
- Option and lease terms of three to five years offered
- One month's free rent

Disadvantages

- Older center; maintenance issues, perhaps
- Depending on who the grocery and drug are, may not be right image
- Space may be too small
- HH income less than other center
- CAM high and not fixed; may be high maintenance
- Real estate tax could go up by a lot
- Because no marketing assessment, may be no marketing plan for center
- No upfitting allowance
- Hours and days of operation not as compatible for Linda's business
- CPI increases could be advantage depending on economy
- Percentage rent, but probably would never have to pay it
- Spouse cosign needed

6. I would like to know the following:

- Who exactly are the tenants in each center, and are they the right image, and are they compatible?
- Where exactly is the trade area for each center?
- What is expected with real estate taxes at North Street Market?
- Can I get an exemption from hours and days of operation at North Street Market?

- Can I get an option at Cabbage Corners?
- Why is CAM so high at North Street Market?
- How is rent determined at option time?
- Roof and parking lot condition at North Street Market (although tenant is not typically obligated to pay for roof replacement or parking lot resurfacing, Linda sure does not want inconvenience of leaky roof or bumpy parking lot)
- Other maintenance issues at both centers. In the CAM clause, exactly who pays for what?
- Exactly where is Linda's space in each center? (Location within a center is important)
- Exactly how (on which sales) is Linda's percentage rent calculated? (On wall coverings, paint, window coverings, but how about labor, consulting fees, etc.?)
- Does she have to use certain contractors or can she use whomever she wishes?
- How is the tenant finish money paid?
- What triggers rent commencement?

Chapter 5 Review Questions Answers

1. **b.** During the due diligence period, the buyer needs to investigate everything that would affect their use and decision.
2. **b.** The letter of intent spells out the "intent" of the business terms to be in a contact.
3. **c.** A confidentially agreement requires the parties to keeps the terms of their negotiations private.
4. **a.** While you could use any of these, the others may leave the boundaries in question or may not be accurate.
5. **d.** Subletting is allowing another to have some or all of a tenant's rights. It is typically allowed unless otherwise stated in the lease.

Chapter 6 Case Study Answers

1. 1,000 sq. ft. × $20 × 6 spaces = $120,000
2. 1,000 sq. ft. (vacant) × $1.50 = $1,500 (can't pass expenses through to vacant space)
3. $120,000 – $1,500 = $118,500
4. $118,500 ÷ 8% = $1,481,250
5. Add to NOI: 1,000 sq. ft. × $20 = $20,000 plus expenses that now can be passed through to tenant of $1,500 = $20,000 + $1500 + $118,500 = $140,000 (new NOI) ÷ 8% = $1,750,000 (new value). $1,750,000 – $1,481,250 = $268,750. A shortcut way to compute this is to look at just the additional income and apply rate: $20,000 (rent) + $1,500 (expenses) = $21,500 ÷ 8% = $268,750. That's a lot of money. Would it be worth someone's efforts to get that space leased? I think so!

Chapter 6 Review Questions Answers

1. **c.** Income properties are best and most frequently analyzed using the income approach.
2. **b.** There must be enough comparables (recent) in the market for this approach to have any validity.
3. **c.** $20,000 – $7,500 = $12,500 NOI per month. $12,500 × 12 months = $150,000 per year.
4. **c.** NOI ÷ Cap rate – Value $150,000 ÷ 8% = $1,875,000.
5. **a.** Interest expense on the mortgage loan is a cost of ownership, not a cost of operations.

Chapter 7 Case Study Answers

Suggested answers:

- How much will be put as a down payment?
- Has the property been maintained?
- What are the terms of the tenants' leases?
- Is there competition nearby?
- Are there new office buildings proposed?
- Who are the tenants?
- What terms is Lamar seeking?
- What is Lamar's financial condition?
- What is the tax and annexation situation?
- Are the operating expenses expected to rise?
- What is the NOI?

Chapter 7 Review Questions Answers

1. **b.** Most life insurance companies use a mortgage banker or mortgage broker as their correspondent.
2. **a.** Banks are the best source for short-term funds.
3. **a.** While banks can make long-term mortgage loans, the assets of a local bank are usually not sufficient to handle a large scale project.
4. **d.** A wraparound loan "wraps around" an existing loan to make a newer, larger loan.
5. **b.** The lender wants to minimize risk and be repaid. While the 10% return is nice, the lender's primary goal is to be repaid.

Chapter 8 Case Study Answers

Suggested answers:

- Exclusive agency (with the existing prospects of the seller excluded)
- Nonexclusive agency
- Open listing
- One-time showing agreement
- Protection agreement (assuming you represent the buyer)

Chapter 8 Review Questions Answers

1. **b.** The commercial information exchange (CIE) lists what a broker has to sell or lease but does not set up cooperation or the compensation. A broker must still handle that separately.

2. **d.** The co-brokerage agreement is the agreement between the firms or brokers.

3. **a.** The exclusive right to sell allows the broker to claim a commission if the property is sold by anyone during the listing period. The other agreements do not.

4. **d.** The buyer's attorney and accountant should provide any legal or tax advice. The agent should provide real estate advice and suggest the client contact their attorney and accountant for any legal or tax advice.

5. **b.** Clients and customers look for someone who has experience in the appropriate areas. They also need to trust their broker and want that broker to be loyal. However, in many cases, a client may pick a broker because that broker is known to them through others or through a common experience such as their country club.

Chapter 9 Case Study Answers

1. Day spa

   Pros:

   - An excellent use for high disposable income area
   - Decent rent
   - Experienced operator with name recognition in town

   Cons:

   - High upfitting ($20,000)
   - Use conflict with nail salon
   - Closed Sunday and in evenings
   - Although hair salon does not have an exclusive, they may complain
   - While it shouldn't be a problem, serving lunch may encroach on restaurant's exclusive

2. Video arcade

   Pros:

   - High rent
   - No upfitting
   - No use conflict
   - Experienced operator

   Cons:

   - Typically unattractive space
   - Typically high turnover
   - Kids running amok
   - Trash on sidewalks and parking lot
   - Probably in need of bicycle racks
   - Lease only if desperate, in most cases

3. Produce market

Pros:

- Excellent fit for high income area
- Experienced operator

Cons:

- New in market, may not survive
- Use conflict with grocery
- Low rent

4. Bookstore

Pros:

- Decent rent
- No upfitting
- National chain
- Good use for demographics

Cons:

- Expense caps on pass-throughs
- Requires exclusive
- Will probably require that you use their lease
- Check to see that drug can still sell paperbacks, etc.

5. Dress store

Pros:

- Great rent
- Local owner who will care

Cons:

- Inexperienced operator
- Wants abbreviated hours
- Upfitting, while not much, wasted if the business fails in the first year

So who is best candidate? Depending on other businesses located in competing shopping centers, I'd lean toward the bookstore, day spa, or produce market. There is an even chance that the grocery won't sign off on the produce market, so they are probably out. I would also guess that the nail salon won't allow the day spa to do nails—that is a deal killer for the day spa, but I would ask. Depending on the amount of the expense caps, I'd look to the bookstore as the best bet. No conflicts, a national merchant, no upfitting, decent rent.

Chapter 9 Review Questions Answers

1. **d.** A broker needs to know all of these and more to best search for the right space of their client.
2. **c.** 2,000 sq. ft. × 115% = 2,300 sq. ft. × \$18 = \$41,400
3. **a.** This best describes some type of net lease. Rent is "net" to the landlord.
4. **b.** This could also be a type of full-service lease.
5. **d.** All of these are just a few of the questions a landlord (or tenant) should ask themselves before trying to go it alone.

Chapter 10 Case Study Answers

Suggested answers:

- Negotiating the purchase of the property/land
- Determining best use
- Finding tenants and negotiating with them
- Secure funding commitment
- Creating conception plans
- Confirming utilities
- Rezoning
- Conducting necessary studies
- Determining overall business climate

Chapter 10 Review Questions Answers

1. **d.** The proper corporate structure would be best handled by the developer's attorney.
2. **a.** The other studies may be a part of the feasibility study. The feasibility study covers it all.
3. **d.** All of these (plus the broker and more) can be part of the development team.
4. **d.** Typically the developer will not look to the broker for financing.
5. **d.** All of these are important when selecting a quality tenant.

Chapter 11 Case Study Answers

Pros:

- Person on site daily
- Can direct their work
- Can use employee elsewhere if not busy
- Employment costs known

Cons:

- When employee ill or injured then you have no one
- Must purchase and maintain equipment
- There may be too much work one week and not enough the next
- May not be property trained or as knowledgeable as a professional contractor
- Need additional liability insurance
- May cost more once related employment expenses added

Chapter 11 Review Questions Answers

1. **c.** The owner's accountant would handle their income taxes.
2. **b.** There are many items the agreement should address. However, the refinancing of the development would not be a typical duty of the property manager.
3. **d.** All of these sources might dictate the need for certain reports.
4. **d.** All of these are good things to consider when deciding how to manage a property.
5. **c.** $32,000 \times 5\% = \$1,600$, which is higher than the base of $1,200.

1031 exchange   An allowed practice under the Internal Revenue Service (IRS) regulations that allows an owner of certain types of properties to exchange them for others and defer some or all of the related capital gains tax.

agency agreement   An employment agreement between an agent and a buyer or seller. Some examples include listing agreements, buyer representation agreements, and dual agency agreements.

air rights   The rights to use the air space over a piece of property.

Americans with Disabilities Act (ADA)   A civil rights law that was passed to prohibit discrimination against persons with disabilities.

anchor tenant   A tenant of an office building, shopping center, or industrial development that has leased a large space. An example of an anchor tenant in a neighborhood shopping center is a grocery store.

big box   Retail real estate slang for large-square-footage tenants such as Walmart, grocery stores, department stores, and Home Depots.

breakpoint   A retail business term that specifies the point when a tenant would pay additional rent based on a percentage of sales.

broker   Used in this book to refer to any commercial real estate licensee. An accurate definition of broker is the type of real estate license a licensee holds. Many states have both sales and broker licenses. Some states have broker licenses only. Some states have different categories of sales and/or broker licenses.

build to suit   A development term describing a building built to an owner's or tenant's specifications. The opposite of build to suit would be a "spec" building. Spec is an abbreviation for speculative.

building code   Local, state, or regional ordinance that specifies the method and materials to be used in constructing improvements (homes, office buildings, shopping centers, etc.)

capital gains   A category of income defined by the IRS which may receive preferred tax treatment. Check current IRS regulations for details.

capitalization rate (cap rate)   The rate of return investors are receiving on similar investments.

cash flow   The cash an owner has left after paying operating expenses and debt service (mortgage payment).

cash on cash return   Annual cash return compared to the value of the real estate.

client   A buyer or seller who is represented by a real estate licensee.

co-brokerage agreement (co-broke agreement)   Agreement between brokerage firms on how the commission will be shared and paid.

commercial information exchange (CIE)   A method for commercial properties to be advertised to other commercial brokers and sometimes to the public. Sometimes confused with a multiple-listing service (MLS); however, a CIE has no offers of compensation or cooperation.

commercial mortgage backed securities (CMBS)   The formal name for conduits.

common area maintenance (CAM)   An expense that can include a variety of property expenses. Typically includes expenses such as utilities, maintenance, parking lot cleaning, management fee, and landscaping expense.

community shopping center   A shopping center that has a trade area of a "community." The area could be 5 miles or up to 20 miles, depending on the other competition.

compaction   A term used to define the ability of soil to compact and support the load of a building.

comparable   Used in appraisal, a comparable, also called a comp, is a piece of property, recently sold, that an appraiser or broker can use as a comparison to the one they are trying to value.

conditional contract   A contract with conditions that must be met before a party has to perform.

conduit   A financing term that describes a method of packaging commercial loans and selling the package in the secondary or other investments markets.

confidentially agreement   Used in a variety of ways. Parties agree that the terms of any agreement will be kept confidential—not shared with other interested parties.

cost approach One of the three approaches to value used by appraisers. Land is valued separately from the improvements. The improvements are priced based on the cost to replace them, with depreciation deducted.

cottage/single tenant office Used in some parts of the country to describe a stand-alone office building for a single tenant—usually small. May be a converted house.

customer A party in a real estate transaction not represented by a broker.

debt service coverage ratio (DSCR) Used by lenders to assume that there is sufficient net income to cover any mortgage payment.

deed of trust One type of mortgage arrangement where the lender holds legal title and the borrower holds equitable title.

deed restrictions Restrictions placed on a piece of property by the seller via a deed.

demographic report Shows census information on an area. Typical categories are the number of households, ages, race, income, etc.

dual agency An employment agreement where the real estate firm represents both the buyer and the seller or the landlord and the tenant. Not an approved practice in all states.

due diligence The process of investigating all of the issues that affect the desirability of a property, such as the zoning and possibility of rezoning, soils tests, feasibility studies, tenant interest, etc.

easement The right to use another's property for a stated purpose.

employment agreement These are agreements between a broker and a buyer for selling for real estate services. Employment agreements include listing agreements, buyer agency agreements, property management agreements among others.

employment base The number and type of potential employees within a certain area.

encroachment Trespass of an improvement. Can be on the owner's property (a building encroaches into the setback) or onto another's property (a building is improperly located over the property line).

end user The occupant of a space.

estoppel certificate A ratification of the tenant's lease by the tenant. Requested by the landlord when selling or refinancing the property to prove the validity of the lease.

exclusive agency agreement A client (buyer, seller, tenant, or landlord) agrees to let only one real estate firm represent them. They may still elect to represent themselves.

exclusive buyer agency agreement Buyer agrees to let one particular real estate firm represent his or her needs.

exclusive right to lease agreement A landlord allows a real estate firm to solely represent his or her interests in a building.

exclusive right to sell agreement A seller agrees to allow only one real estate firm to represent his or interest to sell his or her property.

exclusive tenant representation agreement A tenant agrees to use only one real estate firm to represent his or her interests in an area or region or nationally.

exculpated loan A mortgage loan that has only the real estate as collateral, no personal guarantees.

expense cap The maximum amount a tenant will pay in reimbursement for a specified category.

expense stop Used in leasing to define the limit the tenant or landlord will pay toward an expense.

feasibility study Analyses done to determine whether or not a buyer wants to proceed with the purchase of real estate. These studies may include market trends, demographics, spending habits, analyses of competition and expected competition, economics, etc.

foreign trade zone (FTZ) A designation applied to some areas that allows the tenant (usually a manufacturer) to acquire foreign parts and delay the tariffs until after the item is fabricated. Helps balance cash flow.

full service lease A lease that usually provides full services such as janitorial and utilities. Important to review the lease to see expenses paid by parties.

go dark A slang term describing a tenant space that is no longer occupied because the tenant closed or moved out.

gross lease A broad term used to describe a lease that has the landlord paying for the operating expenses. It is important to read the lease carefully to determine who pays what.

gross rent multiplier (GRM) A way to value some income property by determining value based solely on the income.

ground lease   Also called a land lease. A lease where the landowner leases their land to a user. The user typically constructs a building on the land. At the end of the lease, the lessee may be required to remove the building or allow the building to revert to the landowner.

highest and best use   An appraisal term that defines the use that will bring the best return to the owner. The use must be legal and feasible.

income approach   One of the three approaches to value, commonly used in investment real estate. The property is valued based on its ability to produce income.

institutional investor   An investor who handles investments on behalf of a company, such as a pension fund, real estate investment trust (REIT), or life insurance company.

internal rate of return (IRR)   This calculation measures the financial return taking into account the time and value of money.

joint venture   An arrangement where two or more entities (persons or companies) work together on a real estate investment. It can be in the form of a limited liability company (LLC), partnership, or some other structure.

letter of intent (LOI)   Used in complicated lease and contract negotiations to outline the terms of the agreement to aid in the drafting of the agreement. Not binding.

LIBOR   Acronym for London Inter Bank Offering Rate. Used as in index to determine rates a lender will charge.

lien   A charge against a property or person.

life estate   The right to use a property for the life of some party.

limited liability company (LLC)   A form of ownership where liability is limited to the members but has some of the attractive tax treatment of a partnership.

limited partnership   A form of ownership where the general partner(s) have the liability and the decision making authority and the limited partners have limited authority and liability.

market approach   One of the three ways to value property where an appraiser or broker compares the subject property (the one they plan to value) to those recently sold properties that are comparable. Adjustments are made to determine value.

mineral rights   The rights to mine for minerals on a property.

mortgage   A lien against a property. The owner gives certain rights to a lender in return for a loan (usually a loan to purchase the property).

mortgage broker   Persons or companies who bring a borrower and lender together for a fee.

neighborhood shopping center   A shopping center that has a trade area of a neighborhood or neighborhoods. Usually 50,000 to 125,000 square feet.

net lease   A lease where some or all of the rent is "net" of expenses to the landlord. The lease must be carefully reviewed to determine what expenses are paid by whom.

net operating income (NOI)   Income minus operating expenses.

net present value (NPV)   A calculation that shows the current value of a property (or any asset with some type of income stream) by using the money invested, the time invested, income received, further income invested, an investment rate, and the value at disposition.

nonexclusive buyer agency agreement   An employment agreement where a buyer hires a real estate firm but not on an exclusive basis, that is, the buyer can hire additional firms.

nonexclusive right to lease agreement   An employment agreement where a landlord hires a real estate firm but not on an exclusive basis, that is, the landlord can hire additional firms.

nonexclusive tenant representation agreement   An employment agreement where a tenant hires a real estate firm but not on an exclusive basis that is, the tenant can hire additional firms.

open listing   An employment agreement where a client hires a real estate firm but not on an exclusive basis, that is, the client can hire additional firms.

operating expenses   Expenses necessary to operate a real estate property. Examples of operating expenses are utilities, common area maintenance, real estate taxes, and insurance.

option   An agreement that gives the buyer the choice to buy the property or not under the terms of the attached contract during a stated period. A fee is typically paid.

pass-through expense   Expenses that are totally or partially passed through to either the landlord or the tenant.

pension fund   One of the many investors in commercial real estate. Pension funds use the retirement funds of their members to invest.

percentage rent clause   In some retail leases, this clause allows the landlord to receive additional rent from the tenant in the event the tenant's sales exceed a stated amount.

percolation An older term that is still used to describe a site's ability to absorb water.

power center A type of shopping center that has several large "anchor" tenants.

pro forma A financial analysis of a property's income and expenses. A cost pro forma would be an analysis of the costs to develop a property.

property management Handling the day-to-day operations of a property. Includes activities such as collecting rent, making repairs, completing reports, etc.

property management agreement The employment agreement between a property owner and a real estate firm hired to handle the day-to-day operations of the property.

property manager A real estate broker who manages property for an owner.

protection agreement An agreement that protects an agent's or firm's right to claim a commission, usually from an unrepresented owner.

protection period Period of time in which a firm can still collect a commission after their agency agreement has expired, providing that a named prospect completes the transaction.

qualified intermediary (QI) The party who holds the property or money in a 1031 exchange.

real estate investment trust (REIT) A portfolio of investment real estate structured as a trust. Shares are sold and distributions made depending on the trust's profitability. These trusts must continue to acquire property and will sell properties as circumstances dictate.

regional center A shopping center that serves a region. The region's size and the trade area of the center are dependent on other center locations and the competitiveness of the tenants.

registration of prospects The process a broker uses to claim a prospect as theirs.

rentable A method used to measure space and assign parts of the common area to tenants.

right of first refusal A privilege granted to a party allowing that party to have an opportunity to buy or lease property before it is offered to others.

safe harbor A term used to describe one of the requirements of a 1031 exchange. Safe harbors include a qualified intermediary, qualified escrow accounts or trusts, or qualified security or guarantee arrangements.

sale-leaseback Where an owner sells his or her property to an investor and then leases it back. Used to free capital. May be a good investment for the investor.

standstill agreement An enforceable agreement where the seller agrees to stop marketing the property to others while negotiating with the buyer.

subordinated Means "stand behind." To subordinate your interest means that you will allow someone to stand ahead of you when it comes to claims. Most commonly, a lender will want other interests to subordinate to it so the lender can have the first lien on a property. Some places cannot be traded. In most states the property tax department may always have a superior position.

subsurface rights Rights to any subsurface materials including minerals.

surface rights Rights to use the surface of a piece of property. What we commonly think of when we acquire real estate.

tenant representative (tenant rep) A firm or agent who represents a tenant.

title The ownership interest rights one has in a piece of real estate.

topography The fall of the land. A topographical survey will show the different elevations— where and how the land rises and falls.

transactional brokerage A process where the agents and firms do not represent a client but handle the transaction for the buyer or seller or both. Not an allowed practice in all states.

triple net lease A type of lease where the tenant pays some of the expenses in addition to the rent. In many areas, the "triple" part refers to common area maintenance (CAM), real estate taxes, and insurance. It is important to carefully read the lease to determine who pays what.

underwriting The process a lender uses to analyze the loan. The underwriter will assess the credibility of the borrower, the viability of the real estate, and the likelihood of the lender being repaid.

unsubordinated A classification of agreement, in that the one with a claim on the property does not change places or have to stand behind some others. An example would be "an unsubordinated ground lease." In this case, the landowner would not stand behind the lessee's lender. The lender would stand behind the landowner in the case of default.

upfitting The process of building out the tenants' space in accordance with their specifications. Also known as tenant upfitting or tenant improvements. Frequently the tenant is given an allowance to use when completing their space.

usable   Another way to refer to measured space. With usable space, the square footage reported does not include assessing parts of the common areas to the tenant's square footage.

water rights   Rights of property owners to use water running through or adjoining their lands. The designation of the waterway will determine the landowners' rights.

zoning   Local ordinances that dictate the types of uses allowed on property in the jurisdiction. Zoning can also specify lot size, setbacks, accessory uses, etc.

Notes

Notes

Notes

Notes

Notes